LIVING AFTER THE HOLOCAUST:
Reflections by the Post-War Generation in America

Edited by
Lucy Y. Steinitz with David M. Szonyi

BLOCH PUBLISHING COMPANY
New York

Copyright © 1975, Pages 3-100, RESPONSE: A Contemporary
Jewish Review
Copyright © 1975, Pages 101-114, William B. Helmreich
Copyright © 1976, Pages 115-124, and "Forward"
Bloch Publishing Company, Inc.

Library of Congress Catalog Card Number 76-8322
ISBN 0-8197-0016-9

Cover Photo Credit: Erna Weill

PRINTED IN THE UNITED STATES OF AMERICA

TO OUR PARENTS —
who did so much
more than survive.

TABLE OF CONTENTS

A PERSONAL FORWARD

When I was about ten years old I played a little trick on my mother and jumped out from behind a corner in our New York apartment, catching her by surprise. She reacted with momentary hysteria, instantly regressing to her native German language. It was as if she were suddenly transported back to Nazi Germany, reliving her worst fears and experiences. The incident was never mentioned again. But I learned, through my mother's facial expressions, movements, and references, never to ask questions about the Holocaust. I always remained conscious of the weight behind my mother's silences, the pain behind her memories.

I taught myself about my parents' lives from books, obsessed with novels about Jews during World War II. The heroes of the stories I read began to take on the features of my mother and father, and I became terrified of my parents' world. I tried to imagine myself in their position; would I have had the courage to go on? They had proved their stamina, their bravery, their heroism — I had not, could not, do the same. Once, after a series of minor anti-Semitic incidents at my undergraduate college in Ohio, I tried to draw some parallels between the emotional reactions I was having with what it must have been like for my parents in Europe, one generation ago. Even my involvement in New Left or anti-war activism was partially motivated by my desire to understand (and protest against) the similarities between my own and my parents' childhood environments: the phenomena of mass genocide, human atrocities, and the passivity of the vast majority of the civilian population.

Somehow I harbor the feeling that my life must compensate for the suffering my parents (and millions of others) underwent. I dread, however irrationally, that my parents might one day wonder whether their suffering was all worthwhile. It is as though I am fighting a daily battle against Hitler by trying to insure that my parents' lives have meaning. Since I was young, I have felt that I am not only the child of two people who survived the Holocaust, but the child of all their friends who survived, and of those survivors they didn't know, and of the six million who perished.

Several summers ago I spent two months in Germany in an effort to find clues to my parents' lives. Would Germany treat me differently, I wondered, than it did my parents thirty-five years ago? I was tense, observing every action, ready to hate. But I was given no opportunity to do so — not even in the village beer gardens or while visiting Dachau. Everything was too perfect, and my own ambivalences too great. (*See Hans Herda, pages 125 - 129*). Because the language and mannerisms of that country were so familiar to me from my childhood, I felt very comfortable in Germany. And yet, how horribly different, one generation ago.

In Germany I discovered that the Holocaust happened only because human beings — people who laugh and cry and feel pain like the rest of us — caused it to happen. The most frightening thing about the Holocaust is precisely that it occurred once, and therefore lies within the realm of human capacity to be repeated.

Working on this book was an attempt to articulate many of my feelings about living after the Holocaust. It is the first time the post-War generation has had the opportunity to address themselves publicly to this issue. It began over a year ago when a friend, Dina Rosenfeld (to whom much of the inspiration of this work should be credited), explained how protective she is of her mother. She thought that I would understand what she meant, because she and I are both children of Holocaust survivors. Gradually we discovered that many of our conflicts and concerns were similar. [*See Meyer Goldstein, Anita (Chana) Norich, Dina Rosenfeld, Lucy Y. Steinitz, and David M. Szonyi, pages 33 - 53.*] A strong bond developed between us. I found comfort in the knowledge that I was not struggling alone.

The writers of this volume are young American Jews for whom the Holocaust is not past history. It burns within us, although almost none of us were old enough to remember much of World War II, and most, in fact, were born after 1945. Nevertheless, all of our lives, our theologies, and our collective world view have been affected by the

Holocaust. When we read reports of the atomic bomb, impoverished Jewish communities in Russia, the Middle East, or New York, or of the threat of Israel's annihilation, our memories slip back thirty years. Psychologically, the trauma of the Holocaust continues. There is part of all of us that is survivor; wrestling between hatred and pacifism, depression and hope. This book is intended to provide a vehicle for the sharing of our emotional responses to the Holocaust — perhaps by demonstrating a recognition that we are all partners in the legacy of a post-Holocaust world.

Much of this book is by and about children of Holocaust survivors.

Already an earlier form of this manuscript is being used in a discussion group of children of survivors at Boston University. When some of my own City College students (many of whom are also children of survivors) read the manuscript, they confided to me that they felt "weird, strange, like part of a cult." One told me that she felt as though the book had uncovered her private world.

Sometimes it is hard to talk about the children of survivors because the survivor and the Holocaust itself are still so much with us. It is also difficult to pinpoint particular or unique psychological symptoms attributable to second generation survivors. Only when specific expressions of marginality, depression or anger, guilt, and personality problems come together to form a syndrome may it be identified as typical of children of survivors. Unfortunately, there is very little analytical literature on the survivors as parents or on their children from which generalizations can be made. (*See Erica Wanderman, pages 115 - 123, and Toby Mostysser, pages 3 - 21.*)

The silence of many of our parents has instilled a sense of taboo about the Holocaust from which we are only beginning to emerge. We have only recently gained the emotional distance and perspective necessary in order to look back at what happened. Schools and synagogues have incorporated the study of the Holocaust into their textbooks, classrooms, youth activities, and annual commemorations only in the past few years. (*See Eric A. Kimmel, pages 12- - 31, and Bob Salz, pages 75 - 82*). It is my hope that from this anthology significant inferences can be drawn which may stimulate further research and creative expression. But the manner in which the Holocaust will be finally communicated to future generations — in education, family ritual, social ethics, and through the stories which will become our heirlooms — is dependent on the knowledge and sensitivities of younger people today.

Many of the essays, poems, and illustrations printed here originally appeared in the Spring, 1975 issue of the quarterly magazine, RESPONSE: A Contemporary Jewish Review.* My fellow editors of RESPONSE (Steven M. Cohen, David Glanz, Jon Groner, Leonard Levin, and Nessa Rapoport) worked tirelessly, and, as usual, without compensation. I am very grateful to them. During the nine years of its existence, RESPONSE has maintained its avowed purpose to publish younger, innovative, and lesser-known writers on subjects of Jewish concern. It is through RESPONSE's dedication to high quality, independence, and creative initiative that this book is really possible. I am also thankful to the individual authors who have contributed to this collection, and to Charles Bloch and Debra Goldberg of Bloch Publishing who graciously assisted me whenever I required their help.

Lucy Y. Steinitz
New York City
5736 — December, 1975

*RESPONSE, 523 West 113 Street, New York, New York 10025.

Toby Mostysser

THE WEIGHT OF THE PAST
Reminiscences of
A Survivors' Child

They called it the war, my parents and their friends, on those endless occasions when they sat around and talked about what had happened. Later, in school, I learned about Pearl Harbor and about the Allies and Axis in Europe. But the war my mother and father were in took place in the countryside and villages of Poland, whose names are not on the map, and it was a war against Jews. It couldn't have been before high school or college that I connected that war with the word *holocaust*, an American term, too grand and too remote to touch such a familiar devastation. So I'll call it the war too, because I have come to realize how much it has permeated my own life. I have come to realize this recently and grudgingly.

All the time I was growing up, I couldn't bear the stories my parents told me—or rather the stories my mother told me, because my father generally kept quiet and had nightmares, while my mother relieved herself of the terror by speaking and, oddly, by reliving it.

The worst stories were about the separation of children and parents. My mother was in mid-adolescence when the Germans killed her parents and sister. First her father was taken away. He was shot and then buried in the same grave he had helped to dig. The Germans picked him up one morning when they were rounding up Communists, and collected any Jews who happened to be about. My mother was in her house when this happened, along with my father and her brothers, and they couldn't go outside because they would have been taken too. Some time later the remainder of the family were carted off to a camp. There were the usual selections. My mother's mother and younger sister were shot. My mother escaped the same death only by a fluke, when, with her mother's prompting and a guard's compliance, she ran to the side where her two brothers had been assigned to labor duties. Her mother had worried that without a woman her sons would not be able to cook and care for themselves.

Sometimes my mother would tell me about how as she ran she heard her sister call, "Sarah, Sarah, don't leave me," and how after the war those cries caught up with her and followed her from Poland to Germany and across the ocean to America. Or, she would tell me how she missed her mother, how lonely it was without a mother. That was usually when my father worked late or when, after a quarrel, he would storm out of the house and go for long walks on the boardwalk.

Actually, her own misfortunes were not what she talked about most. Until fairly recently, I didn't know the details of how her father was picked up or of exactly how she was separated from her mother and sister. I mention these things here because, in retrospect, they may explain the rest. Most often, my mother told me about other parents and other children:

— A mother was holding her infant in her arms. A Gestapo officer wrenched it from her and, in full view, dashed it against the ground or against a wall.

— A child was to be taken away and killed. The mother came forward and said: "Take me instead." The soldier laughed and shot the child anyway, and sometimes the mother too.

— A mother suffocated her infant. The woman was hiding with a group of people who were afraid that the baby's crying would reveal their presence and endanger all their lives. They told her that if she didn't kill the baby, they would. She put her hand over its mouth until it stopped breathing.

— A father deserted his son. The two were hiding in a barn when the man heard people coming to search. He ran for his life and left the boy behind.

— Some parents tried to protect their children and fled. They paid Poles to take care of the youngsters, to pretend that they were relatives' children and to shelter them, while the parents fled to the woods, where a child would have little chance of surviving. But when they returned at the end of the war, the child, and sometimes the guardians, had been killed. Poland was full of informers.

Hearing these stories was excruciating. I became the child in every one of them. I was the child my mother had been when her mother and father and sister were torn away from her, the child whose parents fled and abandoned it, the murdered child mourned by its mother, and the child who, just by being alive, murdered its parents. I betrayed and had been betrayed.

I didn't know how to block out these stories. I couldn't cover my ears or turn away my face or even still the turmoil the words created in me. When my mother talked, her words came at me in wave after wave of pain and rage. It was as though her voice and face, driven by energies that did not belong to everyday, were disembodied and filled all the air around me. I would have pushed them away with a huge physical thrust of my arms, to make a cool and quiet space for myself. But I couldn't. I sat immobile. Not until I was well into high school did I tell my mother that I couldn't listen any more, and, then, not seeing the pain I had suppressed, she accused me of not caring about her and left the room.

Not everything I heard about the war was quite so gruesome. Sometimes my mother, and my father too, would tell of victories and escapes, tales whose sheer adventure might have filled me with wonder and excitement had their emotion been less close and less raw. But, as it was, these stories too could pull the world from under me. The one told most often, or that I remember best, is about a party of Ukrainians who came with dogs to search the barn where they were hiding. The men had already discovered and murdered some people, acquaintances, in a barn nearby, and now they thrust their long daggers into the haystack where my parents lay. My father, determined not to die hungry, gulped down the last morsel of bread he had been storing. (He smiles when he recalls this, and my mother cites the detail as evidence of his extraordinary determination and strength of character.) The daggers missed, and the next night my parents moved to another barn, the one where their friends had been killed, knowing that it would be some time before the Ukrainians hunted there again.

In truth, I'm not really sure this is the story I heard. Things were told to me in pieces, and events got mixed up in my head, and I put them together to create an order and a coherence that were never there in the telling or in the hearing. But the details don't really matter. What counts is that my mother and my father and their friends all told survival stories with the greatest awe and bravura. They recollected escapes so unlikely that only miracles made them possible and related feats so remarkable that only the greatest heroes could have performed them.

So these adventures, whose magic should have delighted, also accused me. Together with my mother's greater horrors, they pointed up my own insufficiencies. I had not suffered. I had not survived. I was four years old, or five, or six, or seven, eight, nine, ten, an adolescent, an adult. In some way, everything they told me annihilated the validity of my own experiences and feelings. What childish pain could compare with the pain of seeing one's loved ones murdered, of being hunted, of starving and freezing? I knew even when I was very young that nothing, not the children who made fun of my foreign English and foreign manners nor the bullies in the neighborhood compared with the pain my parents had endured. I was fed I was clothed, I was loved. What did I ever have to complain about? I don't know whether my parents ever raised these questions directly, but they didn't have to. I knew about the war. And I knew for myself that any horrors of my own, any loneliness, or want, or frustration, paled before what my parents had suffered.

And any victory of my own paled before what they had achieved. When I became aware of myself, I began to wonder whether I, in the same circumstances, would have survived. If I was unhappy, I would wonder whether I would have sustained the drive to stay alive through several years of the most abject misery. When I failed at something, whether it was at making friends or at finding a job, I wondered whether I would have had the ingenuity, the skill, the craft, to have kept myself in food and shelter and out of the hands of the Germans, Ukrainians, and Poles. And now I sometimes wonder whether I'm the sort of person miracles would have happened to.

Last, I heard about Rybokova. Significantly, I was not told stories about her, with the usual drama or histrionics, but rather given information. I learned that there was a peasant woman called Rybokova, who allowed my parents to hide in her attic and gave them food—this, in the middle of the war, when she and her children were themselves often hungry, when any prying and malicious eye might have informed on her for a pound of salt or for pleasure, and when, had the Germans or even her own countrymen caught her, she and her family would surely have died a most terrible death. Before this piece of information, I still stand in utter amazement and awe.

Yet, even this incredible example of human goodness and courage could be turned against me. How could I not wonder what I would have done in her place? Would I have risked my life and my children's lives, or even have borne a hungry stomach for almost total strangers, for people who were connected to me only because a tailor sewed and repaired some clothing for me, as my father had for her? Would I have remembered and felt the humanness of pariahs, of people who all my neighbors believed belonged to a race of vermin and parasites, and when so remembering meant opposing my own instincts to the explicit values and assumptions of all the people around me and all the world I knew? When I think about it, I suspect that my parents, having suffered as they did, would not do for anyone else what this woman did for them, but the morality her action embodies has always seemed incumbent upon me, though I never have been one to actively join other people's causes.

The things I heard left me with little faith, in the world or in myself. The world, as my mother depicted it, was filled with more demons than even the imagination of a child could conjure. When she spoke about Rybokova, she spoke with less emotion, less violence, than she brought to the people who had harmed her. Those were unearthly, larger than life figures, whose archetypical malice was the malice of all humanity. As my mother mythologized evil, she made it palpable and immediate. The moral of her stories was absolutely clear: don't reach out, don't trust. The warning applied most strongly to Christians, but it extended also to Jews, to everyone. More than anything else, the sheer evil that was presented to me as Reality, and presented so fiercely, threatened to engulf me. It was always a fight for me, a struggle against my parents and against parts of myself, to press through the demon-filled isolation that I found myself in to the other world of sunshine and people, where I could play and laugh and be easy.

And if the world of my mother's creation was hostile and dangerous, I certainly was inadequate to its challenge. I grew up a mere mortal in a world of martyrs who had suffered, heroes who had survived, and saints who had given. I could have no idea of how I would have behaved in it. Always, I am faced with the spectre of my own insufficiency, and I don't want the opportunity to allay my doubts.

So the war is the mythic reality I grew up with, and it has taken me a long time to acknowledge it as a reality that had anything to do with me. It was mythic because the stories I heard were told to me as myths are told: as primal, symbolic events, without clear chronology, and with barely any of the everyday details that fill an ordinary life. Only recently have I been able to press my parents for clear and specific information and to put the stories into a framework of time and action. But what I was given as a child were the most grotesque incidents, which stood outside of time and space and the human reality that might have made them a little more comprehensible.

Everything my parents told me about happened in a country that I had never seen and that was inhabited by people whom, with the exception of my parents' friends and some of my friends' parents, I had never met. Until I began reading about the war, which was no more than a year and a half ago, I knew nothing about armbands, residence permits, pogroms, nothing about the vast bureaucracy mobilized to locate and exterminate Jews, nothing about the Judenrats or about the organized compliance of the Jewish leadership. Until I read Vladka Mead's book on the Warsaw Ghetto uprising, I didn't know that you couldn't simply move into Warsaw and melt into the stone of apartment houses if you were a Jew, but had to show documents and residence permits so that you could be picked off like a fly. I didn't know that to get forged Aryan papers, you had to produce witnesses, people who said you were a relative, and who were willing to stick their necks out for you. I didn't know that if you ran to the woods, you would be turned in by rightist partisans who fought both the Jews and the Germans in the name of Poland. Not until I read Robert Jay Lifton, who explained the psychic closing-off (so akin to death) that is produced by the extensive presence or persistent threat of death, did I have any inkling of why Jews, as well as all other groups the Nazis persecuted, walked to the collection points, trains, graves, and gas chambers in a haze of docile self-deception or numb indifference—why they didn't fight back.

My father told me some of these things, but not enough. When I asked why more Jews didn't run and hide, he would tell me that they didn't have weapons and that everyone was against them and would turn them in. But I didn't understand the mechanism of how that could happen. My parents told me that Poles could identify Jews by their looks and speech and dress and by their very bearing. But that made no sense to me at all. After all, people in New York couldn't automatically pick me out as Jewish. I didn't see why Polish Jews should walk and talk any more differently from other Poles than I did from other Americans. Though my parents wanted very badly to make me know about their lives, they could not even begin to imagine how much I couldn't fathom. Because they really couldn't know and accept my life, they weren't able to imagine the detailed and specific ways in which it was different from what theirs had been. Sometimes my mother would throw up her hands in despair and say, "American children don't understand anything," and, of course, she was right, considering what she meant by anything. But that only made her angry and resentful and didn't help her to explain.

I was presented not with a history, concrete and semi-intelligible, but with a great, gaping hole. My father sometimes told me stories of his childhood. Rabbis' tales and moral lessons mingled with stories about how poor his family was, about how they often went hungry with nine people to feed, about how he walked miles to school in the snow, and about how he was apprenticed to a tailor at age thirteen and hoped to make good and help his parents. But he has never in my presence named the people who made up his world. I've asked, but I can't remember, how many brothers and sisters he had. The only one I know about in any way at all is the one who also survived, my uncle Meyer. I know that my mother's sister had the same name as my father's mother and that I'm named after them, and I remember being told that my mother's sister had long, blond braids, just as I did until I was about ten. But, except for a photograph of my mother's father which stands on my parents' bureau, that's all. Neither my mother nor my father nor my three living uncles ever speak about the people they lost—as people, that is, with distinct personalities. I never heard about childish games, sibling rivalries, parental conflicts, or any of the things that go to make up a life. All I knew is that they had lost their whole world, their families, the friends they grew up with, the villages they lived in, and the ways they followed. I knew that they had lost everything, but I could barely conceive of what everything was.

My parents could not give me their history, because it had been brutally ripped away from them and was no longer theirs to give. Instead they presented me with a great hole, a great emptiness enclosed by my father's hard and bitter silences and my mother's spoken longing and rage. That hole, I was to fill. Sometimes, when I didn't want to listen to my mother's diatribes about the war or about anything else that may have been troubling her, she would say to me, needing and hurt, "But you're my mother to me, and my sister!" And though I wanted to turn away, I was held by guilt until, over the years, I merged with the roles I had been assigned and learned to feel more comfortable listening than speaking, at least to my parents. I didn't know to ask: if I was my mother's mother, who was mine? How I was to fill the hole and with what, I never clearly understood either. I was instructed to be good and to be pretty, to marry and to have children and a house and money and friends, but I doubt that any of these things would have filled the vacuum. I sensed that I was to create a brand new world, in the image of the old that I did not understand and had never lived in, only that the new world was to be solid, supporting, hopeful, and, ultimately, unreal. I was to live a life of triumphs that no person ever lives. The only thing that I did know for sure was that if I weren't careful, the hole would suck me in.

I have always known how to be careful, how to move, furtively and defiantly, into places the war couldn't reach. Early, I learned how to inhabit my own inner spaces and then, gradually, the world of books and ideas, which, aided and abetted by foreign travel, would, I thought, bring me into regions unspoiled by my parents' nightmares. Their myth, after all, was only a myth; and, on the surface at least, there is a separation between myth and actuality.

By the time I was born, in 1946, my parents had left the horrors of Poland behind them and were settled in the relative comfort of the D.P. camp in Fermvaldt, in the American-occupied sector of Germany. My earliest memories are of Stuttgart, and happy ones. We lived there in a rented room in a large, somber apartment owned by an old German couple. I called them *Uma* and *Upa* Kaiser—my adopted grandparents—and I cuddled in bed with them.

Wolfgang, their grandson, who must have been old enough to be a soldier, used to throw me way up in the air. I liked that. When I was three and we left for America, I promised to send them Maxwell House coffee.

In New York, the war was far away. A few months after we arrived, we moved into a bright, airy three-room apartment, which we shared with my three surviving uncles. In the postwar housing shortage, my parents had to give away a set of china that they had brought with them from Germany in order to get it, but I didn't know that. There were large windows which opened onto the boardwalk and beach. At night, when it was warm, people from the old-age home sang on the boardwalk. On sunny days, I could look out on expanses of yellow sand and of sunlight glimmering on the ocean water. This view of reflected light—idealized, to be sure, and perhaps more a symbol than something that had really given me pleasure—stood in contrast to the dark world of my parents' memories.

Which had nothing to do with my life. My parents saw in America a replica of Europe before the war, where almost every Christian, in the depth of his heart, hated Jews and, given the opportunity, would do everything in his power to harm us. For my own part, I saw hardly any Christians, and in those I did see I could find neither the overt malice nor the prodigious potency my parents ascribed to them. While my parents issued warnings against the *goyim*, I played with Jewish children in Coney Island, where we lived, went to school with Jewish children in Brighton Beach, and grew more and more curious about the nature of the stranger who evoked so much venom and fear. Besides, my own enemies were closer at hand and easier to identify. They were the children who, with exaggerated benevolence, corrected me every time I said "very" with a guttural *r* and who laughed at me when in the second grade I still didn't know the meanings of such household words as "tummy," "brilliant," and "cheesebox," never having heard them at home. Later, we moved to Forest Hills, Queens. I went to Russell Sage Junior High School, Forest Hills High School, and Brandeis University, where 75 percent of the student body was Jewish. These places did little to dispel my notion that the world was inhabited and run by Jews. And if there were any anti-Semites in my midst, they certainly didn't proclaim themselves.

My parents' fears pierced the ecumenical spirit of the fifties and early sixties. "Don't make friends with Christians. When they're mad at you, they'll call you a 'dirty Jew,' even your best friends." My parents claimed to be speaking from experience—old friends turned on them when Hitler came—but it was not my experience.

I came of age in a period of wide-eyed national optimism. People didn't behave the way my parents said they did. On television, civilized cowboys defeated savage Indians and honest cops caught robbers. In schoolbooks, American Democracy fought Communist Oppression, and our government defended the underdog and gave surplus food to the poor, all out of an instinct of decency. The civil rights movement was in its flush beginnings, and we believed that racism could be overcome on freedom rides and in a liberal Supreme Court. The U-2 incident took us in naive surprise, as did the assassinations of King and Kennedy. Our good-guy image of ourselves, with its positive assessment of man's potentialities, was only beginning to tarnish with these events; and when I was in college and graduate school it reshaped itself into the radicals' promise of speedy millenium. For all of its unfortunate simplicity, this world, bright and expansive, was certainly more appealing than my parents' demonic creation, even though I doubted its reality too.

My parents' world was constraining. When I brought friends home, my parents would demand almost frantically: "Is he Jewish?" or "Is she Jewish?" I stopped bringing people home. I wanted to make friends where I found them. Each one, unlabeled, could be a new experience, a new opening to the world. The fact is that most of my friends were Jewish, though disaffected like myself. But my parents would have had me socialize only with Jews. Skeptical of all human motives and overwhelmed by the myriad adjustments their new country required, my parents sought some measure of security in the familiar. I, having little need for that particular kind of safety, found the familiar stifling—especially since it consisted of people with whom I seemed to have little in common, nice Jewish boys and girls who frequented Jewish camps and sometimes synagogues but did little else, people who seemed to have their whole lives mapped out for them. The painful irony of it all is that while my parents invoked the war to justify their prodding, the war had eroded the very Judaism which would have given their restrictiveness some semblance of consistency. Their Judaism, being dependent for its full realization on that community of parents and neighbors which the war had destroyed, deteriorated into sentimentality—a kosher home for the sake of "tradition" and the High Holidays in new clothes at the Young Israel.

I could see little connection between the war and the way we lived. Every few years, my father would have his leg operated on to clean out the shrapnel wound he had received as a soldier in the Polish army. But that was all that was definitive, and it never loomed very important. For the rest, my father went to work; my mother kept house and took in alterations. Then they bought a coat factory and they both went to work, my father twelve hours a day, my mother ten. My father went to work on Saturdays; my mother took the bookkeeping home. They wrenched a good income from the garment industry, invested and saved their money, and bought a house in Forest Hills. They socialized with the refugee community there. There was something genuinely spirited in all of this—a real sense of satisfaction in doing, making, and building, and pride in the recognition they received. I saw a lot of activity, and it was hard for me to reconcile that with the weariness, the downward-pulling weariness, that intruded with every recollection of the war. Though I sensed the unease beneath the busyness, I was too young to perceive in their adamant labor and in their absorption in the things of hand and eye the refugees' desperate struggle to put ground under their feet, a solid ground of both material and emotional security.

Worse, the myth of the war had led me to expect that we should live on a heroic plane. In the war, the only things that mattered were life and death and the means whereby. I knew that. So I assumed that the war would have guaranteed, if nothing else, a clear sense of what was important and what was not. The exact opposite occurred. Appearances clogged our life space. My parents expended inordinate amounts of emotional energy on furniture, dinnerware, crystal, jewelry; on my and my sister's clothing, make-up, hair styles, complexions, and weights—things that other people could see and appreciate and measure them by. They fixated on proprieties, selecting as their social arbiters a small circle of Polish refugees who, along with themselves, tried to resurrect and maintain in New York the shards of the frivolous and hierarchical social structure of Poland. Thus, without being religious themselves, they maintained a sentimental respect for religion and religious people; and when they drove on Saturdays, they detoured around the Young Israel, and they wanted me to make similar concessions. As we settled into the well-off community of Forest Hills, they began to use words like "reputation," "esteem," and "status," as though these attributes were invariably connected with internal qualities. I was baffled. What disturbed me, I think, were not so much specific disagreements on any of these issues, though disagreements there certainly were, but my sense that their motives were all askew.

It was as though they expected happiness, like praise, to bounce back at us from outside; or perhaps happiness didn't even matter but only the right reflection from the mirror-world, which would make them think well of themselves. Even friends, assessed European-style by their family backgrounds, physical appearances, and specific accomplishments, at times seemed to be merely social accessories. Nor is it that my parents are shallow. In retrospect, it is clear to me that the externals were all that the desolation had left them and empty forms were all that they had to build on. When I was younger, though, I thought that the war should have dissolved all such trivialities into nothing.

I understood only what adolescents usually understand: that my parents lived in one world and I in another, that they tried to impose theirs on me, and that it was oppressive. I was at an age when I was hungry for experience, and they had had too much experience. Once, I stayed up all night and in the morning went into our garden and watched the moon fade and go under. My father came out, and I told him how beautiful it was. He said that he had seen too many moons. Then he left for work. I suppose it was all those moons in Poland, when he was running through fields or foraging for food, and the light of the moon was just one more danger to contend with. But I had never seen an early morning moon before, and he spoiled my pleasure.

I needed out. I wanted to meet people different from the ones I grew up with and to know worlds different from the one I knew. At Brandeis, I studied some Spanish literature and learned beginner's French; I took courses in art and music and, freshman year, a class in

African literature, which was as far away from the familiar as I could get at the time. I majored in English because novels and poems opened up other worlds to me and let me get a glimpse of other ways of living and thinking. In graduate school, I specialized in the English Renaissance partly because that seemed to be a world more ordered than my own, and ordered on completely different principles. I wrote a doctoral dissertation on an obscure sixteenth-century poet, Fulke Greville. He was a Calvinist, so my research took me into Calvin's *Institutes* and involved me in book after book of Protestant theology and history.

I wanted to travel. Junior year I went to England, to the University of Manchester, and I spent winter and spring vacations in Paris. A few years later, I spent a summer in Italy, picking up Italian, looking at medieval and renaissance paintings, and playing.

The Europe I went to was not the continent of the war. Germany, where I spent a week refusing to talk with anyone but the acquaintances I was visiting (Germans whom I had met in England), was the only and obvious exception. For the rest, I was going to explore other cultures. In Coventry, I saw the two cathedrals, the remains of the old, which had been bombed by the Germans, and the new and modern edifice built alongside it. On the floor of the old cathedral there was a plaque that told the story. Everywhere in Europe, in England, in France, in Italy, people spoke of the German bombings or invasions during World War II as though they were recent memory. I didn't think to ask about Jews. I looked at old buildings and visited churches, impressed by what a long history everything had. I passed hours in museums and enjoyed seeing so many works of art from one time and one place all arranged together, in a way that I could get a feel for them. I met new people. For the first time in my life I was away from the preponderance of New York Jews I had always associated with, and it was a relief to know people who were casual and free from agonizing intensity. To my parents, Europe was a graveyard. But this was not my parents' Europe.

All of this, both the travels and the studies, were more or less against my parents' wishes. I made some concessions: the choice of Brandeis, a course in Jewish history, a smattering of Hebrew, and a summer in Israel. But, on the whole, I connected everything Jewish with the enormous burden of the war, and I was going to escape.

My parents were apprehensive. They knew I was moving away from where they had been and going to where they couldn't follow. They mistrusted what I would find. Also, they were not a little envious and resentful. I had choices and luxuries which they had never possessed, and they were bitter and proud with the irony that they were helping to provide them. The irony didn't escape me either. I had guilty visions of my parents running for their lives in Poland when they were my age and then in America fettered by young children and grinding labor. But guilt is a motor as well as a trap. I sought freedom and relaxation in otherness.

Then, the Yom Kippur war broke out. I don't want to be melodramatic about it, for that would be inaccurate. Doubtless, the change that took place in my perceptions following the war had a good deal to do with developments in this country. The war in Viet Nam had been dragging on with no end in sight. It had long before eroded our happy image of ourselves. I was teaching at Queens College at the time of the My Lai massacre trial, and I was horrified into speechlessness by the number of my students (since when are college kids supposed to be callous?) who defended Calley. At the same time, the civil rights movement was being perverted into hate-filled confrontations. It came to appear that the rights of one group depended on the negation of those of another. In New York, the antagonisms were being acted out between Blacks and Jews, set against each other by a power structure that maintained itself through the warring of oppressed minorities. Disintegrating was our magic faith in man's capacity for goodness and love.

Nonetheless, the Yom Kippur war was pivotal for me. The '67 war had been short; Israel had gone in and come out on top. In '73 the war was protracted and the outcome uncertain. I saw Israel as small and vulnerable, surrounded by enemies, and quickly deserted by Europe, as in the previous war against Jews. The death toll was mounting, and I felt as though my relatives were dying.

The passion of my response shocked me. It shocked me more than the Arab attack, which was always a possibility in that area. I was amazed by the completeness of my emotional involvement. My general outlook and political opinions notwithstanding, I didn't give a shit about the shades of grey, about the ethics of Zionism,

American imperialism in the Middle East, or the problems of the Palestinians. I cared about survival, the life and death of my people, and of myself. To me, the war was a war of survival, nothing short of that.

I responded to the war exactly as my parents did. And the identification, after years of my going my own way, sent me spinning. Like them, I saw the war in Israel as a re-run of Europe's war against Jews between '39 and '45. It was when Amercan-born Jews I knew didn't react with my measure of intensity, when they didn't merge the two wars into one, and when they didn't immediately see the Yom Kippur war as a war of survival, of their own survival, that I realized I had not escaped my parents' world. I could no longer pursue a delusory innocence. I had to acknowledge their war.

It was then that I first began to recall, willfully and intentionally, the stories they had told me. Realizing that I could not evade their war, I tried for the first time to make sense out of it and to demythologize good and evil. Instead of shrinking from the war, I asked questions. I wanted facts, details, dates; I wanted to know exactly what happened to whom. It was only then that I first learned how my grandfather was taken away with my mother looking on and how my mother was separated from her mother and sister. Prior to that, I had known that my mother's family had been killed, but now I understood something of how close she herself was to their deaths. I read books on the war and on anti-Semitism: Raul Hilberg, Vladka Mead, Bruno Bettelheim, Primo Levi, Elie Wiesel, Hannah Arendt, Eugen Kogen, Hiltgunt Zassenhaus, Martin Gray, Jean Francois Steiner, and others that came my way. These books helped me put my parents' isolated horrors into a context, helped me to understand something of what must have gone on. I began to talk with friends whose parents had also been in the war. We had never discussed the subject before. I realized how significant the common background was in some of my friendships and how much our parents' war had entered into all of our sensibilities. I discovered that while my parents' war was not my life, it was my history, and as such it touched my life. As I acknowledged the war, it ceased to threaten and overwhelm me quite so much.

The Yom Kippur war riveted into my awareness parts of my

own experience that I had tried to tuck out of the way. When the Arabs attacked, I was in the last stages of my dissertation, bored silly by the extensive research I was doing. Calvin had long felt ridiculously alien to me, with his talk of Christ and the trinity, and I had found his harsh philosophy of predestination and damnation perverse. With the Arab attack, I realized how my studies, which were intended to bring me away from the world of my parents' misery, brought me into ludicrously alien regions and, moreover, entangled me in yet another closed system of unhappiness. The attack brought into focus the absurdity of my knowing more about Christianity than I do about Judaism.

My recollections of Europe were also reassembled. I let myself recall that Europe was the first place where I had encountered a casual and taken-for-granted anti-Semitism. In England, you could hear anti-Semitic jokes on the bus, and there were people who would offer the opinion that Jews had started the Second World War. In Paris, people took special note of the fact that you were Jewish if they found out. In Italy, I ran into a *pensionnera* who in a rage one day screamed that Hitler should have finished the job. Also, for the first time in my life, I met Americans who came from the vast reaches of our country where people thought without thinking that Jews were rich, pushy, and clannish. In this Europe, as in most of America, Jews stuck together, in small, tight cliques set apart from their Christian neighbors, something those of my generation in New York City didn't have to do, feeling a secure plurality. On two occasions, at a bus stop in Rome and in a language club in Florence, an Italian Jew came up to me and, out of the blue, asked if I weren't Jewish, clearly excited to have found one of her own. It is not that these encounters with Semites and anti-Semites were frequent—they weren't—but they threw me, suddenly and surprisingly, into a world where one's Jewishness was noticed. I had visited a Europe perilously close to my parents' Europe, and now I let myself know where I had been.

So, here I am. I've acknowledged the war. I have reclaimed it as my history. I have let myself see how deeply it has permeated my entire consciousness, how it has touched every aspect of my feeling and thinking. Now, I don't know what to do with it. Sometimes I look at people on the street, ordinary people, and I connect them in my mind with the ordinary people who murdered Jews, and I wonder what these people would have done and what they're capable of doing. But philosophers have grappled with the problem of evil for longer than I without coming to any resolution, so I shove my questions to the back of my mind, because there's no way I can live with them.

Now that I've accepted the war, I feel that I ought to do something. By my parents' logic, the war requires that I be a "good Jew" and a "good daughter," as though the intrinsic worth of these stances were somehow increased or made more obvious by the war. But here's where the conflict arose in the first place: over my efforts at self-definition and my parents' use of the war as a club to shape me into the shape they wanted.

While I no longer wish to run from everything connected with Judaism, I still don't entirely know what my Judaism means. I have no religious conviction, and the war provides a poor foundation for belief. Hitler's effective racial, as opposed to religious, definition of Judaism made it plain that, for all practical purposes, one cannot choose or reject it at will. In a cultural sense, then, I feel myself a Jew. I feel sensitive to issues involving Jews. I feel drawn to Jews as my people. But place me in a social setting where people congregate as Jews, and I feel like a fraud. As in any group, there are too many individuals with whom I feel little if any personal connection. A common victimization creates only the most tenuous and pathetic bonds. You need to be reminded all the time, to have the face of your enemy visible before you. Yes, I feel a general mistrust of Christians as a group—a primitive and natural fear of otherness coupled with a well-recorded history of brutality and reinforced by my parents' propagandizing. But that barely extends to my daily life. Before actual personalities, categories dissolve. My choice of friends and my genuine feeling for them is not restricted by religion. Their attitude towards Israel and towards other things that interest me as a Jew are governing factors in my selection, as are temperaments and common interests, but not religion alone. I know I'd feel isolated in a place with no or few Jews. Yet I feel ill at ease with the exclusivities of many Jewish groups and their casually accepted reverse prejudices. I want to retain the luxury of meeting people as individuals and the clarity of vision to see each one accurately, to distinguish my friends from my enemies one by one.

Being a good daughter is no less complicated. It would demand countless renunciations beyond the ordinary obligations that one generally has towards one's parents. I'm going on twenty-nine. I'm introspective. I carefully chart the emotional vicissitudes of my days. I churn all sorts of preoccupations about in my head. Too much of my life is internal. I look at my mother and I wonder what I would be like now had I passed through all those deaths, at an age when one is most soft to pain. My own adolescence was not very happy. I was clumsy and uncomfortable with myself. I wasn't popular. I'm the woman shaped partly by those years, when whatever came upon me from outside seemed to constitute the permanent and intrinsic nature of reality, to which one adjusted. I wonder what contours I would have hardened into had reality taken the form of a universe out to annihilate me and every trace of me. I think about my parents and what has been done to their lives, and I feel compassion for them. I marvel at all they were able to do despite that and at how little cynicism they have, considering it all. I'm tempted: "They suffered so much, I should...." Then I stop. Otherwise, I would lose myself. My parents don't like my lifestyle: unmarried, living in a grubby apartment on the Upper West Side, involved in psychotherapy, women's groups, and all sorts of other things they don't understand or accept. This is not how they would have wanted to live. The things I do don't fill them or make them feel worthwhile. They would write scenarios for me, and I would act the petrified roles they would have played if ...

My action must lie elsewhere. To begin with, I think it's necessary for me to disentangle the historical occurrence of the war from the way it was transmitted to me. As history, the holocaust involves all Jews and seems to call for a more or less political response: the defense of Judaism, Jews, and a Jewish State; the control of technological violence; the teaching of the holocaust—in short, making sure that destruction never again strikes us as a people defenseless and unaware. The transmission of the war was a more personal matter, involving my parents and myself. It created personal anxieties and conflicts, and the healthy response seems to be to try to resolve them. What do I do? I reject imposed guilt. I mean it when I say that I didn't start the war, couldn't have stopped it, and can't undo it. I stop measuring myself against my parents and their war. I insist on the separate validities of their lives and my own, and I fully believe that mine is no less worthy for having been less traumatic. I allow myself to feel happy.

In truth, I've only just begun to exorcise the demons. In reading about the war, in talking about it, and in writing about it, I feel as though I have usurped my parents' experience. I still feel both the guilt and the triumph of the usurper. But in taking possession of their war, I've changed it, so that while their war remains theirs, mine, being second hand, is a separate upheaval. Perhaps with this wedge of difference, I can eventually accept the war and myself both.

"Prayer," Erna Weill, Sculptress

Eric A. Kimmel

THE DISTANT SMOKE
Children's Literature and
The Holocaust

This actually happened. The confirmation class had just finished listening to a harrowing account of the war-time experiences of my friend, Mrs. Rose Zar, who fought with the heroes of the Warsaw Ghetto, knew Mordecai Anilewicz as a friend, and was practically the only one among her family and friends to survive. Rose has often given this talk, because unlike some who find their experiences too painful to relive, she believes it important that our young people be able to hear what happened from the lips of someone who was there.

Even so, despite Rose's considerable wit and poise, the first question from the group left her speechless.

"Why do you always tell us the Jewish side? How come we never get to hear the German side?"

Is it shocking that a fourteen-year-old Jewish child could ask such a question in the religious school of an Orthodox synagogue? Perhaps at first it is, but not after you think about it a while. You see, for the average American Jewish child today the Holocaust is hardly any more real than the land of Oz.

And why should it be? For most of our children poverty and hunger are abstractions, things which haven't touched their families in two generations. Anti-Semitism is equally long ago and far away. A social snub or perhaps a few angry words exchanged on a playground is the extent of it. The children of college-educated professionals have been taught all their lives that there are two sides to every issue; that tolerance is next to godliness; and that the Deity, assuming He exists, is undoubtedly a liberal Democrat, someone along the lines of a divine Adlai Stevenson. *Fiddler On The Roof* is the past, *Exodus* is the future, and Harry Golden enlightens us about our present condition. Convinced of the benevolence of Heaven and the rationality of our neighbors, we are sleek, smug, sometimes self-pitying, but always self-indulgent. And this, for the most part, is reflected in our children.

Consequently I have often felt that the attempt to teach such "kinderlach" about the Holocaust is a task every bit as awesome as Moses' effort to make a brave, free people out of the former slaves of Pharaoh. What are we asking? We are asking a child whose greatest crisis so far in life has been making the swimming team to comprehend a world where a man's life is worth less than the fillings in his teeth; where responsible civil servants tally up heaps of eyeglasses, dolls and empty shoes; where uniformed officers dine on vegetables fertilized with human ashes, wash their hands with soap made of human fat, and sleep peacefully at night on mattresses stuffed with the hair of murdered women. It is a world without pity, without justice, without honor or meaning or sense or any sign that the good, loving God who supposedly cherishes his people Israel exists. Adults who lived through it even today cannot comprehend it. What then are we going to ask a child, a sheltered, pampered child, to understand?

Simply this. That not so many years ago the legal government of a supposedly civilized nation declared the Jews to be vermin, like rats or fleas or cockroaches, and had them killed as efficiently and as cheaply as possible. The rest of the world stood by and let it happen because, quite simply, no one cared to get involved. The Jews who died, weak, frightened, confused, were people like you and your family; people who looked like you, thought like you, and in many cases were related to you. But for an accident of time and place another child would be sitting in your chair, sleeping in your bed, wearing your clothes while you would be just a bit of dusty ash blown by the wind across a field in Poland.

What we must create is not so much an absorption of detail as a changing of consciousness—a very difficult thing to bring about.

The way that is most often attempted and which most often fails is that of history. The assignment of chapters and the inflicting of quizzes to force the memorization of names, dates and numbers is thoroughly pointless. A statistic is not a human being; a map is not a life. Shock is sometimes used to drive the message home. Certainly photographs of bodies stacked like cordwood leave a more lasting impression than mere numbers, but I sometimes wonder whether we tend to overestimate their long-term effect, especially on a generation that regards a monstrosity like *Night of the Living Dead* as a form of entertainment. Horror is a cheap commodity these days, and even were this not the case, its effectiveness is still highly limited. We watch the films of the bulldozers shoving the corpses into the trenches at Buchenwald. At first we are sickened, frightened, appalled. Then we simply become numb. The bodies are stiff, ghastly puppets, decaying meat to be quickly covered. These are not people; these are things, no more human than the bulldozer. There is nothing to feel in all this hideous landscape. Therefore, after a while, we feel nothing.

Children need to feel. In order to understand they must be able to reach out to another human being across the barriers of time and death and fire. Only in the touching of their hands, the children of the future with the children of the past, will the shadow of the twisted cross be shattered forever.

How does this come about?

Through books.

In recent years many juvenile books have appeared dealing in whole or in part with Holocaust themes. These books, however, vary considerably in content and tone, but even more important, in their basic understanding of the tragedy engulfing the Jews of occupied Europe.

Ironically the most exciting and numerous category, the Resistance novels, are also from the Jewish point of view the most superficial and consequently the least relevant. The problem is simply that in books of this genre Jews are seldom main characters, and the dangers Jews face are seldom explored in any great depth. Instead, rescuing them too often seems like merely another bead in a rosary of obligatory adventures: fool the Gestapo, print the underground newspaper, murder the collaborator, rescue the downed British pilot and—oh, yes, almost forgot—save the Jews. The fact that the Jewish characters are totally helpless and incapable of offering anything but platitudes in the way of resistance only further serves to reduce them to the level of stock figures.

This is not to say, however, that these Resistance novels are bad books: quite the contrary, they are extremely exciting and fast-paced with unusually good characterization and feel for the period. It is just that anyone seeking vivid Jewish characters is not going to find them here.

There is, however, one exception: Yuri Suhl's magnificent *Uncle Misha's Partisans*. In this book, based on the exploits of actual bands of Jewish partisans operating behind German lines in the trackless forests of Belorussia and the Ukraine, the men and women of Uncle Misha's camp strike back fearlessly against the murderers of their friends and families. The most memorable episode is probably Motele's penetration of the German officers' club and his planting of the bomb, but I was far more moved by the midnight discovery of a collaborator's house, stuffed to the rafters with clothes and furniture stolen from murdered Jews, even a wedding dress which Lyuba, the partisan girl, recognizes as her sister's.

If *Uncle Misha's Partisans* has one flaw, it lies in the fact that for some unaccountable reason (he certainly knows better) Suhl is overly kind to the Ukrainians and the Soviet partisans, giving the impression they fought together with their Jewish friends against the common enemy. In actual fact they ran a close second to the Germans in callousness and cruelty. However, this flaw fades into insignificance in light of the book's most outstanding aspect: that to date *Uncle Misha's Partisans* is the only book that presents proud, Yiddish-speaking Jewish fighters going off to battle with guns in their hands and the ringing words of the Partisan Hymn on their lips.

> "The victory was small, but oh, how sweet!
> A victory for the Freedom day."

Unfortunately Jewish Resistance is as rare in juvenile books as it was in real life. The more commonly found pattern involves families or individuals trying to save themselves. Sometimes they succeed, sometimes not.

Those who managed to get completely beyond the reach of the Nazis had the best chance of survival. For some this involved having connections, money, and nerves of iron. For others it was largely a matter of luck. The Refugee novels include both extremes, but for the most part these books are concerned not so much with hair-raising escapes as with the day-to-day life of ordinary men, women and children trying to cope with the problems of building new lives and new hopes in countries not their own.

The Jews of the Refugee novels are quite different from the ones in the Resistance books. Where the latter were helpless and poorly-defined, these are resourceful, strong, vividly portrayed people. In fact, characterization is the strength of the Refugee novel, largely because of the fact that they are either admittedly or implicitly autobiographical. Judith Kerr, Sonia Levitin and Esther Hautzig spent their childhood as refugees, and their experiences and their families form the respective core of *When Hitler Stole Pink Rabbit, Journey to America* and *The Endless Steppe*. Whether the crisis is Anna's struggle to master the French language or the Platt family's long, desperate wait to hear from Papa in far-off America, or Esther's sudden transition from a comfortable home in Vilna to a crude exile's hut on the Siberian frontier, we cannot help but feel that these are real challenges met by real people. Consequently, while the Refugee novels might not provide much in the way of high adventure, they are nevertheless moving, penetrating books that leave a far deeper impression than some of their more exciting rivals.

However, their impact is nowhere near as great as that of what might be called the "Hiding" books. These books deal with families unable or unwilling to flee while the opportunity still existed. Now they are trapped, but at least they have the presence of mind not to be caught in the open. The Hiding books have a great deal in common with the Refugee books. Both are strongly, if not completely, autobiographical and are marked by vivid characterizations. However, in the Hiding books the oppressive, claustrophobic atmosphere seems to make everything more forbidding and intense—as if the action were taking place inside a pressure cooker, which, to a considerable extent, it is.

The Hiding book par excellence is, of course, *The Diary of Anne Frank*. Some might point out that the *Diary* is far more than a juvenile book. I agree, but only to a limited extent, because the *Diary of Anne Frank* speaks to the hopes and dreams of young people with such beauty and clarity that they have taken it and treasured it as one of their own.

What gives the book its impact is the ever-present tension

between the delicacy of Anne's words and thoughts and the horror that lurks just outside the bookcase door. The reader is in a strange, uncomfortable position. He knows more than the author. He knows that Anne, so beautiful and loving, is going to die, and that her death draws closer with every page. It is an unsettling thought, to think of Anne Frank naked, dead and rotting among the corpses in the pits at Bergen-Belsen. Yet that is what the Holocaust is: that thought, multiplied six million times.

Johanna Reiss' *The Upstairs Room* has many similarities to Anne Frank's *Diary*, as the story of two Dutch Jewish sisters who go into hiding in the upstairs room of the Oosterveld family's farmhouse. The tension, the fear and the boredom are everpresent here also, but the fascinating relationships between Johan Oosterveld, his wife Dientje and Opoe his mother serve to relieve some of the pressure. That, plus the fact that the children do manage to survive, makes the total impact of *The Upstairs Room* far less than that of the *Diary*. It is a book for a younger, less sophisticated child.

Some Jews, the majority in fact, neither fought nor fled nor hid. They merely waited, hoping somehow that the terror around them was all part of a bad dream that would go away once they opened their eyes. When they opened their eyes it was too late.

Hans Peter Richter's *Friedrich*, written with insight and feeling no less remarkable for the author's being one of modern Germany's outstanding children's writers, is easily the most harrowing of the books in this group. What Richter makes crystal-clear is the point that the Holocaust was no mere pogrom, no sudden, impulsive flash of violence. It was an elaborately planned, systematically carried-out symphony of violence, diabolically contrived to soothe its victims at the same time as it drove them further and further along the path to death. Through the eyes of a German child we learn how the Jews, represented by Friedrich and his parents, are gradually deprived of ordinary human dignity, of the means of earning a living, of police protection, or property, and when nothing else remains, of life. Friedrich, once a happy boy with many friends, dies alone in a bombing raid—a hunted, terrified creature, denied even the right to cringe in a corner of an air raid shelter.

By contrast the terror in Marilyn Sach's *A Pocket Full of Seeds* is as quick and as clean as a surgeon's scalpel. The Niemann family, living in the hurricane's eye of Vichy France, finds it hard to believe that real danger exists. So great is Mr. Niemann's certainty that the war is going to be over in a few months anyway that he cancels their planned escape to Switzerland. The Gestapo, however, functions right to the end. Nicole, the eldest daughter, comes home from spending the night with a friend to find the little apartment ransacked and the family gone. The last chapters of *A Pocket Full of Seeds* form a bitterly ironic parallel to the Resistance novels, where everyone seems ready and eager to help the Jews. Nicole, stunned and desperate for a place to hide, finds the doors of former neighbors and friends slammed in her face. It is Mlle. LeGrand, a schoolmistress, generally regarded by the town "patriots" as a collaborator, who finally takes her in.

But what of those who were not taken in, who entered the transports bound for mysterious "resettlement" camps somewhere in the east? I only know of one juvenile book which follows them that far, and then, only part way.

This is Marietta Moskin's *I Am Rosemarie*, which takes a Dutch-Jewish family from Amsterdam to Westerbork and on to the dread Bergen-Belsen. The Brenners endure all the torments of killing labor under the guns of bestial guards, miserable food, disease, and the overhanging despair that they will never leave the camp alive. Yet they are lucky. Somewhere along the line they have acquired Latin American passports, just pieces of paper, really, stamped with the seal of a country they've never seen. Yet it is enough. The Germans, who care nothing for human beings but have a great respect for pieces of paper, exempt them from the transports leaving Westerbork. It is not until the latter part of the book that Rosemarie, finding her dying friend Ruthie among the prisoners evacuated from Auschwitz when the Germans abandoned Poland, learns what happened to those thousands of frightened people whom she saw herded into cattle cars with whips and ferocious dogs and hauled away toward the east for "resettlement."

That is as far as we go. To date no juvenile book has yet confronted the ultimate nightmare in the manner of Andre Schwartz-Bart's *The Last of the Just* or Elie Wiesel's *Night*. But are clouds of poison gas enveloping screaming, naked people, bloody teeth yanked from the blue, gaping jaws of corpses, quivering bodies hurled into blazing furnaces—are these subjects for a children's book? Yes. And in the case of Jewish children, absolutely! Because if our children do not feel, they will not understand, and if they do not understand they will forget.

And if they do, the sin on our heads will be greater than the sin of Cain. Cain murdered his brother. We let ours be forgotten.

Bibliography

(All the following books were used in preparing this article, though all were not necessarily cited. For a more complete discussion of the Resistance novels I refer readers to an article of mine entitled "Confronting the Ovens—The Holocaust and Juvenile Fiction," which will appear in *The Horn Book* sometime in 1975.)

Benchley, Nathaniel. *Bright Candles: A Novel of the Danish Resistance*. New York: Harper & Row, 1974. Grades 7-12.

Frank, Anne. *Anne Frank: The Diary of A Young Girl*. Translated by B.M. Mooyaart—Doubleday. New York: Modern Library, 1952. Grades 7-12.

Hautzig, Esther. *The Endless Steppe: Growing Up In Siberia*. New York: Thomas Y. Crowell, 1968. Grades 5-8.

Kerr, Judith. *When Hitler Stole Pink Rabbit*. Illustrated by the author. New York: Coward, McCann & Geoghegan, 1971. Grades 4-8.

Levitin, Sonia. *Journey to America*. Illustrated by Charles Robinson. New York: Atheneum, 1970. Grades 3-6.

Moskin, Marietta. *I Am Rosemarie*. New York: John Day, 1972. Grades 7-12.

Reiss, Johanna. *The Upstairs Room*. New York: Thomas Y. Crowell, 1972. Grades 4-6.

Richter, Hans Peter. *Friedrich*. Translated by Edite Kroll. New York: Holt, Rinehart & Winston, 1970. Grades 4-8.

Sachs, Marilyn. *A Pocket Full of Seeds*. Illustrated by Ben F. Stahl. Garden City, N.Y.: Doubleday, 1973. Grades 4-6.

Suhl, Yuri. *Uncle Misha's Partisans*. New York: Four Winds Press, 1973. Grades 4-8.

Wuorio, Eva-Lis. *Code:Polonaise*. New York: Holt, Rinehart & Winston, 1971. Grades 5-8.

Wuorio, Eva-Lis. *To Fight In Silence*. New York: Holt, Rinehart & Winston, 1973. Grades 5-8.

The following materials, though not specifically intended for a juvenile audience, will be of tremendous value to anyone seeking to give children a fuller understanding of the period.

Berwick, Michael. *The Third Reich*. New York: G.P. Putnam's Sons, 1971. One of the best discussions of the Hitler era and the Final Solution available for readers of junior high age. Well illustrated with photographs.

Kantor, Alfred. *The Book of Alfred Kantor*. New York: McGraw-Hill, 1971. A chilling reproduction of the author's drawings of scenes of camp life in Terezin, Auschwitz and Schwarzheide. Kantor was a prisoner in these camps during the war.

Glatstein, Jacob, et. al., eds. *Anthology of Holocaust Literature*. Philadelphia: Jewish Publication Society, 1968. A fine collection of stories, poems, memoirs and documents of the Holocaust era. Excellent for reading aloud even to younger children.

Grossman, Mendel. *With A Camera In The Ghetto*. Tel-Aviv: Ghetto Fighters' House, 1970. Actual photographs of life and death in the Lodz ghetto under Nazi rule. An invaluable and heartbreaking record taken by the photographer at the risk of his life.

Songs of the Vilna Ghetto. CBS S 63345. A recording of some of the most memorable songs of the Jewish Resistance movement, including the Partisan song forming the leitmotiv of *Uncle Misha's Partisans*. In Yiddish, with a printed translation provided.

Suhl, Yuri. *They Fought Back: The Story of Jewish Resistance in Nazi Europe.* New York: Crown, 1966. Stirring accounts of the courage of Jewish fighters in the ghettoes, forests and camps. Highly recommended for reading aloud.

Volavkova, H., ed. *I Never Saw Another Butterfly*. New York, McGraw-Hill, 1964. A moving collection of poems, stories and pictures by children in the Terezin camp where, in addition to some semblances of civilized life, classes in writing and drawing were permitted. Much of the children's work survived the war. Most of the children did not.

"Yartzeit," William Aron, Photographer

Five Children of Survivors: A Conversation

Thirty years after World War II, the memory of the Holocaust lingers with us. For most survivors, it has a daily effect. It also influences the thinking of the children of Holocaust survivors. Five of us, all in our twenties, got together in January, 1975 to discuss this part of our heritage. We wanted to examine the extent to which our "Weltanschauung" is determined by the World War II experiences of our parents and families. Much of this is guesswork. We found that perspectives we thought were unique, were in fact common to the whole group. More significantly, in our minds these perspectives were a result of the direct role the Holocaust played in our childhoods.

MEYER GOLDSTEIN recently began working as a Legal Aid lawyer in New York City.

ANITA (CHANA) NORICH is a graduate student in English literature at Columbia, and is studying Yiddish literature at YIVO.

DINA ROSENFELD is a social worker and a member of the New York Havurah. She was on the editorial board of the special RESPONSE magazine issue, "The Jewish Woman: An Anthology" (Summer, 1973).

LUCY Y. STEINITZ is Coordinator for Academic Development in the Department of Jewish Studies at City College of New York. She is especially interested in the problems of the Jewish aged.

DAVID M. SZONYI is a doctoral candidate in Jewish history at Stanford University, whose dissertation deals with the works of Emil Fackenheim and Elie Wiesel.

DINA: My mother was from Czechoslovakia and my father from Romania, where my parents got married. Both my mother and my father were in concentration camps; they both had families before the war. Both their spouses and the children died during the war. My parents got together and got married after the war. Thus, their experiences have been of both concentration camps and work camps, as well as losing children, a wife, a husband, parents and siblings. After the war, each went back to his or her home town to see what remained, and because little remained, they established new homes in different cities. In Romania my father was persecuted by the Stalinist regime until his death in 1954. We lived in Romania until 1959 and, after spending a year in Israel, came to America in 1960.

LUCY: My mother was fortunate to emigrate from Germany before the war and came via London to the United States in 1940. My father, who (like my mother) came from a fairly assimilated German-Jewish background, was in France before the war. There, he became involved in leftist politics. He fought in the French army for a short period and was taken to a French concentration camp, escaping from a second camp into Switzerland. After the war he came in 1947 to the United States as a foreign correspondent for a year-long assignment, but met my mother and stayed in the U.S.

ANITA: My parents are both from Lodz, Poland, were both in Polish and German concentration camps during the war, and afterwards were in DP camps outside of Munich, (where my brother and I were born), where my father was DP camp administrator. Before the war, they were both active in *Poale Zion*, a Socialist-Zionist workers' organization. We came to the U.S. from Munich in 1957 and have lived here ever since. The only surviving members of my father's immediate family are a brother living in Israel and a sister in Canada; he lost his parents and two brothers. My mother lost her mother (her father died before the war), a sister and a brother. She has only a few distant cousins remaining.

DAVID: My mother's side of the family is from both Switzerland and Germany. My mother was born in Switzerland, but moved to Berlin when she was a very young girl and lived there until August, 1939. Her family was able to get out of Germany just before the war because they had kept their Swiss citizenship. I've just learned that in 1931 there was a big argument within my mother's family over whether or not they should adopt German citizenship. Only at my uncle's insistence did the family retain Swiss citizenship. Because of that, they were able to get out at the last moment and it is also because of that—a decision made 18 years before I was born—that I'm alive here now. My father, who was born and raised in Budapest, left Hungary in 1938 because of the quotas against Jews in Hungarian universities. (There was already a fascist government in Hungary even before the war.) He came to Zurich to study, and met my mother there. His parents remained in Budapest, and were among the thousands of people slaughtered and buried anonymously when the Germans evacuated the city in December, 1944. My parents lived in Zurich, where my sister and I were born, until 1953. That year, they emigrated to Montreal, and came to Philadelphia a year later.

MEYER: My mother escaped from Danzig sometime between 1939 and 1941. The only part of my mother's family, which was fairly small, that was lost was a brother of hers, killed trying to flee the invading German army in Russia. My father was raised in Malavna, a small town outside of Warsaw, where he went to a yeshiva. During the war, he was in different concentration camps and from 1945 to, I think, 1948, he was in DP camp in Italy. In 1948, he came to the United States, met my mother, and they were married.

LUCY: There are only two American-born among the five of us, Meyer and I. Also, we come from small families—I think three of us are only children. That's partly a result of our parents' having married late in life.

DINA: Perhaps we could describe the atmosphere of our homes as we grew up: what were the effects and the implications of our parents being Holocaust survivors? Did the shadow of the Holocaust permeate our lives and, if so, to what extent?

MEYER: I'm particularly interested in the extent to which our parents spoke about the Holocaust directly and explicitly. In my situation, my father rarely spoke about it, only occasionally mentioning a certain incident. He also never expressed any bitterness or hostility toward the Germans in particular. My mother, who didn't go through the camps, was more vocal and outspoken.

LUCY: My family situation is very similar to yours, Meyer. I'm constantly amazed at the goodness of my parents and at their forgiving attitude. But there's something I find difficult to understand: my father returned to Germany in 1947 to give a lecture and wanted, as I understand, to become a part of the reconstructed government under Adenauer. He felt that the needs and realities of post-war Germany should override his personal feelings—that Germany would continue, and that therefore the Holocaust had to be dealt with and understood. He also felt that people would do whatever they could to prevent another holocaust from taking place. My father is editor of *Aufbau*, the German-language weekly started by and for refugees in 1933. He has always been involved in newspaper work, particularly for German and Swiss newspapers, and sees himself and *Aufbau* as links connecting Israel, Germany, and the United States. In my home, perhaps with some reluctance on my mother's part, there were constant associations with Germany (where my father often visited—and my mother and I also after I was fourteen). I always grew up relating to Germany, toward which there was never any particular animosity, although, strangely, I have more blocks in some ways than they do.

MEYER: What about your father's experiences in camps—was that something he'd ever discuss?

LUCY: No, neither of my parents discuss it and somehow I can never bring myself to discuss it very directly. Just this fall, for the first time, my mother told her story about living in Germany in the late 30's. These things have been so well buried that neither they nor I are able to bring in the additional suffering and tears. I feel that's been my loss but can never bring it upon myself to cause the pain again.

DAVID: I'm glad you mentioned pain—maybe that's the real reason why my parents never talked about the Holocaust; there's a real emotional taboo about it: a sense, especially with my father, that if you ask him about the Holocaust or about his parents, you're evoking tremendous pain. The pain might come out through something like watching films related directly or thematically to the Holocaust. My parents have talked more about the Holocaust in the past several years. Perhaps they've been encouraged to do so through some of my interests—I'm working on a dissertation on Elie Wiesel and Emil Fackenheim. Also, I've approached the topic very gingerly, and asked them not so much about the Holocaust *per se* as about their childhoods.

DINA: It's interesting that you say that now they're talking about it more. I think that has a lot to do with age, with it being thirty years after. When I was born, my parents decided never to mention the Holocaust. After my brothers and sisters were killed, I was the new beginning. They were going to forget all the pain, the past, and start anew, have faith again, I guess. That maintained itself for a long long time. Now the situation is very different: the older that my mother gets, the more she recollects, not because we sit and talk about it (we never sit and talk about it because I don't want to hear it from her) but because almost everything will spark off a memory of the way it used to be. Only two years ago, my mother put up, next to my pictures in her bedroom, a picture of her first daughter. In terms of asking stories in the home itself, I tried to find out everything I could, but always did so through books; I read everything I could possibly get my hands on, but I would never ask—*never*—; that was taboo.

LUCY: Was the reason, again, that you didn't want your mother to suffer more than she already had?

DINA: I didn't want to suffer more either—it wasn't just a matter of saving her the agony. You see, it's one thing to read about it and sit there and cry about it, but to actually hear that this is what happened to my sisters and brothers—it was too much to bear, something I wasn't able to do, so I preferred to hear it from a book.

ANITA: That's similar to what I remember. I know a fair amount about my parents' experiences, but only because I've pieced together sentences. It's incredible what children remember: I can remember things from when I was eight, nine, ten, which I just stored up somewhere and then, when I was thirteen, I'd hear another incident and suddenly it became a whole story. I've heard the same thing from other people with a similar background. I can piece together a number of incidents, incidents I mainly hear from my mother. My father doesn't say much—I just know that he was liberated from Dachau but don't know specifics. But my mother has five or six incidents from which I've heard installments over a period of twenty years or so. Finally they fit together into a whole story. It's not the kind of thing that I would ever sit down and ask about; even when I hear half-sentences I don't pursue them, even though I want to. You get information from books and Israeli museums, not by renewing pain.

DINA: One more effect of the Holocaust on our growing up: dreams. Even though I don't think very much about concentration camps and Germans in my daily conscious life, I had recurring nightmares in my childhood—they sometimes reoccur—of various scenes of say a truck with herded-up Jews pulling away, or hiding underneath the bed. A lot of this I don't remember being told, but I might have been and stored it, and they're recurring themes which make me re-examine the whole issue.

ANITA: One thing I'd like to bring up that I've always had a very serious objection to is the use of the term "Holocaust." I thought I was the only one, but I've met many people with the same kind of objection. I never knew that the Second World War was called the "Holocaust" until I was fourteen or fifteen—until I was old enough to know better—and then it appeared in a book that somebody in the family had. I always thought it was almost a sacrilege to call it the "Holocaust," because I didn't really know what the word meant. I looked it up in the dictionary, there was a clear concept which could be defined and limited. To have called it "the War" without specifying *what* war because any fool knows what you mean—gave it more of that sense of mystery it always had whenever it came up in my house. To call it "the Holocaust" gives it a kind of definiteness that makes it seem as though we understand what we're talking about; which we don't really.

MEYER: I'm not sure I accept your reason, but I've always felt a little uncomfortable with the term too. There was a time when everyone was calling it "the Holocaust," as though some PR man had decided we should have a new term for it. I use it because we all know what it means, but whenever I say it, I feel as though it's somehow artificial.

DAVID: There may be a relationship between our discomfort with the word "Holocaust," (or with any word that describes what happened to the Jews between 1933 and 1945), and our inhibitions about talking to our parents. The problem is one of speech and language: I think there was a real gap between our asking about the Holocaust and our parents answering. We were asking in terms of searching for information about our past, trying in some way to relive something our parents had gone through. Our parents in answering were feeling something that's far beyond the power of words to either convey or contain, painful beyond words, and—if it's not a cliche, "traumatic."

LUCY: Our parents' not telling us has to go hand in hand with the question of how much we asked them. I've asked next to nothing, like Dina. I've also worried about my own suffering in their response. I want to *know* very badly, yet, I dread the moment of having to raise the issue, although I realize that it is my duty to learn and to be able to retell their story to my children.

MEYER: That ties in to a couple of points I wanted to make. The only time I ever asked my parents was when I was taking a course on the Holocaust. I decided that I was going to use that as an excuse to fill in some personal details to the objective facts. I don't think it was a conscious decision not to raise the issue—somehow there was just this gap that I learned at some very early age not to approach. I didn't know whether that was to spare myself pain or because of the fact that they didn't approach it. Somehow I learned instinctively. My parents, or our parents, have never integrated it into their own lives; I don't know if it's the kind of thing that one *can* integrate into one's life—that's why I see their reluctance to raise it.

ANITA: There's a Yiddish expression that sprung up after the war. When you wish someone good health, you say "You should live to be 120." Only after the war, it became a kind of gallows' humor, a DP camp joke, to say "You should live to be 126." Why 126?—because the six years of war obviously don't count. There's a real sense of gap there. I can ask questions and I do about my parents' life before the war, before concentration camps, even about ghetto life—and I know details about after '45, how my parents met again, how they were rejoined, how they got married, even about DP camps. But there's a real sense of six years that are simply not there.

DINA: On the six-year gap: I definitely feel those six years all the time, and also feel that they have entered into our everyday life. For example, if something has gone wrong and my mother or I are upset about it, my mother will say, "The kind of mistakes that were once made were worse. When I didn't hide my daughter, that was a real mistake—everything else is really nothing in comparison." Another example: talking about someone's virtues or qualities, my mother would say, "The real virtues or qualities would come out in who was really a *mensch* in the Camps, because there it was done to the very bare bones, and nothing else counted but that kind of thing."

DAVID: I'd like to discuss the relation of the Holocaust to our parents' sense of living in America. Because my parents had a sense of being persecuted and chased through Europe, they really wanted to become very Americanized. They looked upon America as a new start, and wanted to have a security here that the history of the 30's and 40's had denied them in Europe.

ANITA: Coming to America—the question that David raised—does include a sense of a new beginning. It is the kind of thing that Dina said about her birth being a new beginning. I think it's the same thing with all of us, even if we're not first-born children: there's a sense that each new child is in fact a real new beginning. Coming to America is the culmination of that. There's a real appreciation—something that I sometimes think is grossly overdone—for the values of American life, its freedoms to get a good education, earn a living, support a family, and have simple quiet more than anything else. And yet in some sense there's a real disdain for some American values, things that are dismissed as "American idiocies"—*Narrishkeit, idiotisch*. Why do people live the insane way they do now?—it's "American," our parents might say. Somewhere, there's an inability to balance those two feelings about America. When I talk in my own unpatriotic way, it annoys my parents immensely, because they say, "Where else could you have gotten this kind of life? Where else could you have all these things? —which is probably true. On the other hand, they're glad that I'm not a real, "full-blooded American;" there's a kind of pride in my acceptance of a European background, my desire to know about that background.

LUCY: You've noted how we've learned "instinctively" not to talk about the Holocaust. I'd like to pose the question: how did we learn to be different, that we are children of survivors? How is that a kind of special category of Holocaust victims? What kind of experiences did we have as children that did bring us to this attitude? I think the term "instinctive" is the appropriate one for me as well. Also, I share David's and Anita's ambivalence about being "European." I recall walking in Washington Heights and seeing my parents frowning at other people speaking German because "this is America after all." Yet they were very conscious of peoples' roots. There was a special sense of pride when a poor immigrant boy had made good, particularly if that person were Jewish, especially German-Jewish. But basically everything was very private. Not only were the six years never publicly spoken of, but there was a kind of inner reference to it which stayed within the circle of the family.

MEYER: Without being able to point to anything definite, I've always wondered how I'm different because of the Holocaust, in the sense that my parents went through the Holocaust—this, other than the fact that I'm a first-generation American, the son of immigrants. Perhaps being the children of survivors includes a whole cluster of distinguishing traits which makes us different from native-born Americans; I'm not sure that it's simply the Holocaust that I see as a distinguishing factor. In the community in which I grew up, there were very few Holocaust survivors—people who'd actually been through the concentration camps. Besides my father and one or two other people, I can't recall being exposed to that many.

LUCY: For me, the distinction came when I went to Germany, or when I went "back" to Germany. There, I felt that, except for a tragic accident of history I would be living in Germany now. Furthermore, had my parents not been Jewish, I would have been on the Other Side. That's terribly frightening. My motive for returning to Germany is not really sorted out in my mind. In part it was a questioning, and a search and a wondering, "What is my country?" I felt that, except for this thin line, I might have to feel very guilty; it was a horrible kind of feeling.

DINA: I was raised in a community where everyone's parents had been through the Holocaust, so that it was a common experience. For example, I really didn't realize that people had grandparents until I came to Israel and America—that that really is a possibility for Jews.

ANITA: Dina, weren't you always especially surprised that there were also grandparents who were born in America? It was O.K. for my friends to be born in America—how old were they after all? But for people's *parents* to be native-born, and especially people's grandparents . . . I was fifteen before I was able to accept that, and I still have trouble with it. That's a real culture shock. Whatever grandparents were around were sort of "adopted;" I had "adopted grandmothers" at different stages of my life.

DAVID: I also felt the Holocaust's impact through relatives—or lack of them. One of the things I associate with America is Norman Rockwell paintings, with their *heimish* sense of the family together. I have a sense of my relatives being scattered all over the world. They didn't just gradually move apart, but were suddenly "blown apart" through this event.

ANITA: Does that affect the way we think of our family: our surviving relatives? Three and a half years ago I went to Israel, more than just to go to the Jewish homeland. I was nineteen at the time and had never met my father's one surviving brother. I think we take pilgrimages to meet these people—to Chicago, to Canada, to Israel. My greatest urge now is to go to Australia because I have cousins there.

DINA: I very much associate with what you've said. I've gone to Rumania, Hungary, Israel, Canada making these "pilgrimages," trying to piece together my life in some way. In addition, because of the lack of relatives and siblings here, I've tried hard to make my community of peers an extended family.

DAVID: I want to talk of questions of religious faith. When I talk about the Holocaust, I feel like I'm in what the Germans call a *Sackgasse*, a kind of dead end: there's no right response. I feel anger and resentment at God, don't see how the traditional Jewish conception of God can be reconciled with the reality of the Holocaust. So in some ways a belief in God seems absurd to me. At the same time, to account for all that happened in non-supernatural, historical terms seems even more absurd to me; the fact that this incredible suffering could not be given some kind of meaning seems absurd and terrible. So I guess I waver between those two kinds of absurdities and feel a constant dialectic between faith and non-faith, faith and very sharp breaches of doubt.

MEYER: I haven't thought of my faith or non-faith as somehow attributable to the Holocaust. Somehow faith as some kind of intellectual or even mystical thing seems somewhat alien to me, something I have difficulty with. In terms of Jewish practice, the Holocaust has made me more aware of being a Jew; call it "culturally" or whatever, I know that it's very much part of me. In some ways I can divorce the whole faith question from that of religious practice.

DAVID: But do you think Judaism is there "in your bones" more from the Holocaust. I mean would it be there equally from something like Zionism or other Jewish influences?

MEYER: I don't think so. It's not the Holocaust as an intellectual symbol or emblem that has any meaning to me, because I don't know whether I relate to it at all on that level. But it's part of my family history, and in that way has a certain impact. Intellectually, I agree with Fackenheim's "Don't give Hitler posthumous victories," but somehow that really doesn't have much to do with being a survivor's son. Somehow it expresses itself in identification and practice. I'm not sure what kind of identification and what kind of practice—it's a question on which I've gone through different sorts of cycles and different sorts of responses.

DINA: I go through the same kind of separation of faith and cultural practice. In terms of faith, the Holocaust had a major effect in making me feel pretty close to an atheist, although "atheist" sounds too extreme. Still, the only way I relate to God is through anger. Sometimes I yell at God, scream at Him, complain to Him—why was He such a @†$%! to have made the world in such a way, to create human suffering. But I never think of Him in any other way but complaint, and His being guilty. On the other hand, I primarily identify as a historical Jew, not just in terms of the Holocaust, but as an Eastern European Jew, the culture of the *shtetl*, the pictures of my grandfather with a long beard and my grandmother with a *tichel* on her head. They're me, part of me; to deny their background is somehow denying myself, saying that somehow I did not exist before I created myself after college graduation, when I discovered that I was a separate entity. Yet that's nonsense, because obviously I'm a continuation of all these various kinds of people who've gone before me.

LUCY: For me the Holocaust has been the most determining factor in my life because it was the most determining in my parents'. We've learned to live with the absurdity, perhaps much better than people who haven't had to confront it as directly. On the one hand, I feel very Jewish, keep a kosher home and identify in other traditional ways. On the other hand, I'm out of words and arguments against God or His existence or at least His *Chesed*, loving kindness. I think our situation has forced me to confront this absurdity at a relatively early age; I was dealing with these questions when I was 11 or 12 years old, much earlier than any of my peers. Being a child of survivors made that dialectic between faith and cultural attachment present in my home.

ANITA: Meyer used the term "intellectual response." Yet my response to much of being Jewish, and especially to the Second World War, is not at all intellectual: I respond on an irrational, emotional level, which is part of my problem in speaking of "the Holocaust." We're using the kind of terms we do in our classrooms and work lives, with our friends, and that's something that we just can't do with this. Responding irrationally is the only way I know how to cope with it.

LUCY: I once spoke to my father about Emil Fackenheim's statement that one can't give Hitler posthumous victories by giving up one's Judaism. In a way that's affected my thinking, my father answered that one can't give Hitler the credit of having changed our lives; of *making* us Jewish. I've never known quite what to do with that. His whole philosophy is to live his life as normally as possible and really fight any influence—religious, philosophical, or other—that

Hitler might have had to change him.

ANITA: That's very noble, but I don't know if it works.

DAVID: I tend to think—and this is just impressionistic, that the Holocaust tended to take away or put breaches in people's faith. It rarely made unobservant people more observant. However, the Holocaust has had a very strong ideological effect—and that relates to Zionism. Perhaps one valid generalization we can make is that our parents' generation does not respond to Zionism rationally or intellectually: Zionism has a certain existential necessity for them. They feel committed to it with the special fervor of survivors.

LUCY: My parents would take exception to that; they're non-Zionists.

DINA: There's a very sharp split in my family. The observant side of the family asks: "What other kind of response can you make in the face of this absolutely un-understandable phenomenon?"

ANITA: My freshman year at college I took a religion course taught by Theodore Gaster. He developed the whole idea of the two-sided personality of the Jewish God. There is *Yahweh* or the avenging God, and there is a benevolent God who "watches over His flock." I had never heard that divison put quite so clearly. I started to relate that to the Holocaust. For a long time it was unbelievable, and I struggled with the same kinds of religious questions that we've been talking about. Is there a reason for this? Is it part of God's plan? Is there something to which I can relate intellectually or emotionally or at all? In the end, however, I wound up completely rejecting this concept.

LUCY: In my Christian college we learned that the avenging God died with Jesus.

MEYER: So that's where He went.

ANITA: So He was gone before the War? That's comforting to know. When I was younger I gave up the questions of meaning, and now I've come back to them. Where does God come into the war? Is this part of His plan? Is this punishment for sins? Is this an avenging God testing His people—I went through that for a number of years. After a while I gave it all up and said this is *nonsense*; this is historical tragedy and not divine intervention in any way. Now that I've become more involved in Jewish religious affairs, I've come back to the point of accepting part of it.

DAVID: I want to talk about something important in my life—politics. I've been in several sit-ins against war-related campus recruiters at Stanford. Stanford is a well-off, fairly WASPy school, and at demonstrations a disproportionate number of the demonstrators are Jewish. I thought a lot about why this is so, and found myself instinctively making comparisons to the "ordinary German" in the Third Reich. I tried to put myself in his or her place: to ask what would I have done and how bold would I have been? Then it occurred to me that I'm not a German, but for reasons unknown and seemingly arbitrary, I felt an obligation to do something, now, even if I was doubtful as to the efficacy of protest. Maybe I and a lot of people there, as Jews (and particularly as post-Holocaust Jews) had a sense of the contingency of our lives and the reality of mass suffering for others. We wanted not to be in silent complicity, as so many people were in silent complicity under Hitler. I remember one protest where the president of Stanford was present, and tried to dismiss the demonstration. Suddenly, this Jewish professor shouted at him, "How would you have responded if you'd been president of a university during the Third Reich and Krupp had come to recruit?" I could see from the president's face and gestures that he really didn't appreciate the question. Glancing around, I could see that the Jews present had understood and *felt* the impact of the question, were able to relate it to their own presence there.

MEYER: In some ways, I'm really uncomfortable with that. On the one hand, I do feel the Holocaust has made me sensitive to the whole question of responsibility and silent complicity. On the other hand, I find statements like "We can't be silent now because the Germans were silent during World War II" a simplistic connection—or maybe it's the connection in the first place that bothers me, saying that the situations are equal.

DAVID: I'm not saying that.

MEYER: I know you're not. To try to make my point personally relevant: I know I haven't made that connection in politics or whatever. I'm not involved in every humanitarian cause that comes along. I ask myself in what ways I am overlooking my responsibility to the rest of the world. Am I doing the same thing the Germans did? Still, I feel trapped within my limited resources and the amount of time I have to devote to different causes.

LUCY: I'd like to relate to the whole area of responsibility and suffering psychologically. Somehow I've grown up with the world view that one is only allowed to exist if one has suffered; that is, I'm only allowed to live if I have suffered. Perhaps this comes from the example of my parents and my parents' friends. Certainly that is their life story. I have to "suffer" by trying to alleviate suffering for others. And because my parents have suffered so much, I feel I can't bring additional suffering on them. Similarly, I feel I was brought into the world to try to alleviate the kind of suffering other people are undergoing, whether in Biafra or Bangladesh, or resulting from another kind of political or natural disaster. Also, I feel that I can never complain about my own troubles because when compared to what my parents went through they're nothing. I don't have the *right* to suffer. By thrusting myself into some kind of self-sacrificing, anti-bourgeois lifestyle, I'm allowing myself to live in the only way I've been internally taught.

ANITA: The similarity of our responses is surprising. I've felt what you've just said too. I also want to relate to what Meyer said about silence and complicity. I have always been extremely uncomfortable in the whole political arena, because of the huge mob, say in front of Low Library at Columbia in '69. There were lots of famous speakers and people our age standing around with a great deal of enthusiasm, and clenched fists raised—that always scared the hell out of me. When people would jointly chant "Stop the war now!," I was never able to respond. All my friends thought I wasn't politically committed, but I could never respond to mobs. Whenever I heard arguments by Jewish friends about silent complicity, I also felt deeply annoyed; war was one thing and the Holocaust is another—we all know the arguments so well. Still, I feel our involvements now are partly due to some kind of silent comparisons to the Second World War.

DINA: I was somewhat involved in campus politics. I could always go to meetings and do this and that, but I could never shout in unison with a group. I still can't, even for a Jewish cause like an SSSJ meeting. It always reminds me of the fear of the mob scene, the mob lynching. Last summer in Montreal, I went to a kind of German beer hall. When everybody banged his mug simultaneously, I couldn't stand being there. My friends were very committed Jews, but really didn't respond in the same way. One more political thing: I grew up in a Holocaust survivors' neighborhood, Borough Park. I was always surprised at the conservatism of the people, especially in relationship to blacks and other persecuted people. Their view was "Well, nobody helped us—why should we help them?" That has always bothered me a great deal; my attitude has been "Since nobody helped us, this is our chance to reverse that pattern." I was raised in one kind of atmosphere and I came to a totally different conclusion from that with which I was brought up.

ANITA: I want to discuss the Israeli image of the Holocaust and Jewish resistance. It was something that shocked me when I went to Yad Vashem and Yad Mordecai, and other memorials to those who died in concentration camps and ghettos. I knew of the Warsaw and Treblinka uprisings—my mother's sister died in Treblinka—but I was amazed at what the memorials were lauding: valiant people fighting against an enemy, "they were outnumbered, without arms, getting the worse end of it, but *fighting*—this was a battle," these memorials all say. That upset me, because those pictures and monuments seemed to be saying that we were engaged in a war and we lost. It amazed me that this is what one would want to emphasize. Though there were uprisings, resistance groups, battles, these weren't the main responses, nor are they the point.

DINA: I identify tremendously with what you're saying. I've always been offended by the terminology of going to the gas chambers like "cattle" or "sheep"—I always resented that terminology, the sense that everybody who didn't revolt was a "sinner," didn't count. Of course the overwhelming majority did not revolt. But by feeling this I thought I was really "negating" the Israelis' existence or something. I was teaching the Holocaust in Hebrew school—teaching Hebrew school you really get an idea of what is essential to you—and I compiled a booklet of Holocaust literature. Those people I presented as heroes were those who'd created a culture in the various ghettos. Though the world was falling around them, they held concerts and maintained schools.

ANITA: My father was active in organizing schools in the Lodz Ghetto. I always felt pride that he was involved in that kind of resistance movement. But once, in scanning names of people who were active in the armed resistance, I came across a name I recognized—a brother of one of my parents' friends. There was a real sense of affinity and identity in finding that familiar name.

LUCY: My father is a kind of spokesman for the German-American-Jewish community, and I feel that as his only child I'm carrying that weight one generation further. One of my goals is to try to perpetuate his tradition. How I'm going to do that I have no idea. Should I marry and raise a family, I don't know how I'm going to transmit any of this. I feel it's also given me a drive and motive, something about which I feel good.

ANITA: I'd like to stay with your point about continuation, Lucy. I was named after my mother's mother and I've always felt that she was really continued in me. That's a really powerful Jewish symbolism: it's not simply giving a name as a token of respect—it's a really powerful continuation. I *am* my grandmother in some incredibly non-rational sense. There's not only that eastern European life that's continued in me, but there's a real soul that is somehow reincarnated in me and to which and for which I am responsible. There is a story that goes with this. My real name is Chana. My mother took me to school when I was five years old. But she was told that in America you can't be called Chana. My mother, not knowing how to respond, said "Oh." The next-door neighbor she took along as a translator said " 'Anita' is a lovely name," so who knew from English names?, and I lived with "Anita."

MEYER: We'll call you Chana in *Response*.

ANITA: I wish you would; it'd be a whole new beginning. The importance of naming—what was the first thing that Adam did?

DINA: My Hebrew name is "Serifka" which was my father's mother's name. When I was really young and my father took me to services, people would couchy-coo me and ask "What's your name?"; I used to say "My name is Serifka from Orhay." I was never in Orhay in my life, but my grandmother lived there. This was my identification—my grandmother reincarnated. Now when I think of various things that have happened in my life like giving speeches somewhere or having my name appear in print, my mother would always say, "So, Serifka from Orhay—you've really proved yourself." My friends use it sometimes too, as if they're saying "So, Serifka from Orhay, you're a *Mensch*."

LUCY: What we're discussing now is not at all unique to the Holocaust, but has been institutionalized within Judaism for generations.

ANITA: Dina has this wonderful theory in which she's a *Nachas* machine cranking out *Nachas* all the time. When you achieved something you'd "made it" for them.

DINA: It's a kind of reparations to our parents, that element of "making it."

ANITA: Not just for your parents, although that's probably the major part of it because they're there, but to really continue the tradition and have "done them right."

LUCY: And you can't afford to let them down, to fail.

MEYER: Three of us are only children. That, combined with the whole survivors' syndrome, puts us under tremendous pressure.

ANITA: That, a feeling of family dependence, for example, is not unique to us as children of survivors. We simply put it in those terms: when we think of moving away, we think of the losses our parents have had. "How many losses can you impose on them?" In an American society whose major quest is for independence, that's a really difficult question to pose.

DINA: The issue is self-fulfillment as well as independence.

ANITA: Yes. There's a real tension between the American quest for self-realization and the ties that we are *compelled* to feel for our families. Reconciling the tension between being independent and finding fulfillment and meeting parents' expectations is something I haven't been able to do. Trying to make certain breaks while maintaining ties to home has been an impossible thing to achieve. The reverse is also impossible. I still can't figure out how we reconcile being children of survivors, and yet adults and professionals in America.

DINA: The most support I've gotten on this question has always been from children of other Holocaust survivors. To so many other friends, it seems as though I'm carrying something on my shoulders and not really fulfilling myself. That's really difficult.

ANITA: Isn't it abnormal to go home so often?

DINA: . . . and be involved with one's parents so much. It's a failing in *you* that you're not as independent as you should be.

DAVID: I think we've known many people who've made total breaks with their families.

ANITA: And I've always found that very shocking . . .

MEYER: I sometimes have a certain envy . . .

ANITA: Perverse?!

MEYER: Yes, but it's a kind of freedom . . .

DAVID: While I don't want to put a damper on this discussion, I wonder if at times we don't over-attribute things to being children of survivors. I think much of the closeness of the Jewish family, and mutual anxieties between parents and children, comes from Jewish history in general and the culture in particular.

MEYER: Perhaps part of the syndrome of being a survivor's child is that one doesn't always know where to draw the line in attributing things to the Holocaust or not. It can become a convenient rationale for our actions.

ANITA: Whether we over-attribute or not, when I think of independence, I think of it in terms of my parents' experiences, even though that's different from most of the rest of the world's perceptions. There's a real difference in our perception of ourselves. Many Jews are like us in terms of affiliations, ties to parents, siblings, relatives, world-view. But we—or at least I—perceive of ourselves differently, have this often depressing sense of our own background that's difficult to come to terms with.

MEYER: While we were talking about our feelings of religion and politics, I was feeling a certain anxiety concerning our ability to articulate and discuss these things. Perhaps I'm over-attributing again, but for me one of the results of being a survivor's son is that it's made me very private in certain kinds of ways, both in terms of certain Jewish activities, and in terms of political demonstrations and other events. Somehow I see it as having made me closed-up about certain aspects of my Jewishness.

LUCY: How does that relate to the way we make and have friends? Do we find it as easy to make friends with people who aren't children of survivors? How do we relate to non-Jews?

DAVID: I find it almost as easy to become friends with Jews who aren't children of survivors. But for me the real chasm is between Jews and non-Jews. I've often wondered if there is such a thing as a collective historical memory, something people instinctively understand about each other even without the words "Holocaust" or "War" being mentioned. For Jews, I think that such a collective memory exists. There are certain assumptions that we share.

ANITA: In the past few years, I've had many experiences with children of survivors, and there's a kind of ease of understanding—no one has to justify the problems of independence and family closeness, for example, some of the things I refer to are understood, almost before I say them.

MEYER: In the past two or three years, the two or three people with whom I've become close—and this has just occurred to me here—were also children of survivors. That doesn't at all mean that I can't have non-Jewish friends, or friends who aren't children of survivors, but there is this certain spontaneity with survivors' children. In some ways, I think we instinctively know who we are; I can go into a room and immediately know who's "one of us."

DAVID: I think your phrase "one of us" is interesting. Perhaps as Jews after the Holocaust we still have this tremendous sense of vulnerability, something recent Jewish history has reinforced.

LUCY: With regard to your phrase "one of us," Meyer, I have a sense based on our discussion tonight that there's a separate sub-community of Jews, and we're all a part of it.

DAVID: But what happens with the next generation? I worry about how we're going to talk about the Holocaust to our children. We know about the Holocaust intellectually—through books and films among other things—but we also "have" the "Holocaust" in our nerves a little—through our parents. But that's not going to be true for the next generation. Right now, most schools, even Jewish ones, don't teach about the Holocaust. We've talked about the danger of facile analogies, about overusing the word "Holocaust" and over-referring to it, but I also think there's been the opposite tendency: the Holocaust has been mystified, called an "abyss," a unique historical event—perhaps that is one thing that has contributed to the popularity of a man like Elie Wiesel. Perhaps people mystify the Holocaust so as not to have to deal with it. We need to develop certain types of commemorations and rituals, though I haven't thought how that can be done beyond things like Yom Hashoa (Day of Remembrance). We have to give the next generation at least a little bit of the visceral sense of the Holocaust we felt in our generation.

LUCY: I sometimes think that we do both the Holocaust and ourselves an injustice by making it into a Jewish event, by saying that it was 6 million Jews who died, as opposed to 25 or 50 million people. In the next generation the nearness and personal identification with the Holocaust won't be present. We will have to place the Holocaust back into history, and that's difficult.

DINA: While I'm not sure how this ties in, being a child of survivors, I somehow feel that it is essential that I should have children. Somehow continuity becomes much more important for children of survivors, for the sake of *Veshinantam levanecha*, ("You shall teach them to your children.").

MEYER: I guess I don't see myself as being more successful in trying to transmit the story of the Holocaust to my children, because that's even more difficult than something like ritual observance, which can be "learned" through practice in the home. But the Holocaust is such an emotional thing—how do you transmit it in any kind of conscious way?

ANITA: Our parents didn't try to transmit it in any kind of conscious way either; it's just part of them the way it's part of us. I'll probably follow my parents' example and tell it through their stories and through the reminiscences of how they affected me.

DINA: But it's not part of us the same way it's part of them.

ANITA: That's true.

MEYER: I think most of us will have much more the facade of mainstream Americans of one kind or another. Internally, we will be different, but we'll be successful, career-oriented, middle-class . . .

ANITA: Unemployed.

*　　　*　　　*

In the four months that have passed since the initial taping of this conversation and the production of the final edited version, this article has been read and revised several times. We apologize for the occasionally abrupt transitions in the article. We attempted to make it as short as possible without doing too great an injustice to many of the issues we believed were important.

We have seriously questioned the merits of such an article. Have we anything unique to say? Are we truly representative of survivors' children and therefore qualified to speak for them? Are we over-attributing our personal concerns and dilemmas to the horrors our parents survived? The answer to each of these questions is, we believe, a qualified "no." We neither think we have offered profound illuminations on the condition of survivors' children, nor do we claim that what we have said can speak for all who share our backgrounds. But we and future generations will have to consider the continuing effects of the Holocaust and the influence it has had on our lives. The reflections in this article represent our attempts to come to terms with the very personal responses we have necessarily made to the Holocaust.

"Job," Erna Weill, Sculptress

Enid Dame

DIASPORA 4

I remember history
class. WW II
staved off until spring
then blitzed in a week
and us polished off
in a footnote.
The teacher would say,
"Any questions?" By then
I'd learned not to ask.

Was the teacher
embarrassed? I was.
Even when she was a Jew.
Even when she wasn't. Even when
I wasn't, the subject embarrassed.
We avoided it like a bad smell.

No one
would admit a thing.
Not even my parents
those ecumenists
who, nevertheless,
put on wild seders:

Those nights were different!
We'd assemble metaphors:
an egg, a bone, a washcloth,
a root. I'd ask the questions.
Dad kept finding various
socialisms hid in the haggadah.

We'd all grow hilarious
over sweet wine.
Mama said, "It's our rite
of spring, of rebirth.
All religions have them."

We never acknowledged
those German uncles and aunts
disappeared into history.

We never
called ourselves
survivors.

They said, "All men are brothers."
They said, "Get good grades."
They said, "Don't ask us now.
We'll tell you when you're older."

(Older,
I'd learned
not to ask.)

Now
I sort through metaphors:
a mogen david dangles
from my left ear,
a mezuzah hangs from my nose,
a seder plate squats
on a Jiffy hook
over my bed.

A question
for survivors:
What constitutes
an adequate gesture?

Yesterday
my Irish-
American husband
threw roses on
the grave of the Warsaw ghetto
in Riverside Park.
A survivor spoke
to him. Not to me.
I was fumed
in a hot stuck subway
for hours. When I got
there, it was over.

Later, we
drank tea in glasses
and seltzer water
and felt inadequate.

What
should I do now?
Learn Hebrew?
Learn Yiddish?
Learn the Kabbala?
Learn the dreidel game?
Chop off my hair?
Pick oranges in Haifa?
Picket anti-semitic rock operas?
Force my nice
goyish husband
to convert?

In a world
of survivors
is any gesture
adequate?

Michael Waters

DACHAU MOON

1

There is a place like Germany in the body
that wants to remain a secret,
where all the tremendous weight of a life
is a kiss buried in the eyes,
pale moons that drift like heaven
across this bastard landscape

& I am flying to this place
on an overcast morning
when nothing is ready to rise,
so it's easy to imagine a moon
blue & romantic as a dead woman.

This country is full of surprises.
My parents have told me to keep an eye
for the family star,
the remains of dark bone charcoal
thumbed like a mole
on the left side of the forehead.

2

Three days in Munich
and my head begins to split,
the beer tastes like a railroad
& I have been too fucking polite
like a child come home from death.

I am astonished by the number of gold teeth
taken from the mouths of the dead
and placed in the heads of fine German women.
There is a beauty in gold
when found in a dark forgotten place

and a fear
when the moon resembles a gold tooth
lodged in the skull like a light.

The smile of the engineer is a killer,
precise as a military operation,
all the way to Dachau.

3

The stillness is so complete
not even the dead are here anymore.

All the fathers are gone,
having kissed their daughters like fever,
to a room where the moon is seen as a face
blue and almost romantic in mist.

So unlike the photograph in the museum:
someone, maybe an uncle,
strapped in a chair
with his forehead neatly sliced
& opened like a jewelry-box,
the brain and its still water
exposed to the hands . . .

His mouth shapes a small *o*
that could be a moon
disappearing for the last time.

4

The sad Jews
who may be our fathers
haul themselves across New York City
as if weighted with stones,

& in my pocket is a stone
selected that day in Dachau
that contains all the darkness of a family

and I remember the moon is a skullcap
not placed properly on the head
like this, Lord, like this.

Gershom Gorenberg

INTRODUCTION

I met them

when I was twelve, in my grandmother's living

room. They stared

at me from a fifty-five year old photograph.

She spoke

in a voice as low as wind

rustling through trees in a Russian village cemetery

(do not ask me how I know. I know).

"My brother. They made him dance on hot coals.

My brother. They shot him.

My brother. Beaten.

My brother. Hung.

My brother. Knifed."

I made no more sound

than tombstones.

62

Liliane Richman

JEW'S COMPLAINT

Adam's daughter too proud
Has no patience, no time
no desire to convince the neighborhood
Hardware seller, bloodied aproned butchers,
Benjamin Franklin's salesladies
Marmorean bank tellers
and the orange street guard
Crossing muffled ears to safety,
And you my sister, ma soeur.

Won't you strip to the primeval
organ grinder's tune?
"Show us, show us, show us
Ain't you really different underneath?"
Will not display Flesh and Limbs
Lampshades in grim awed museums.
Turns down the defender,
"Not her, she's OK, a friend of mine
One of them, but different, White."
And two-stepped unafraid
Shook her head, not sadly
Too much like you
too much unlike you.

Page boy, paper boy, soft haired boy
What do you bring
When darkearly you walk the morning route?
Kernels of her inherited nightmares,
Father Zeus' banal idea
head borne, ready shoed in shiny soft black boots?

Adam's daughter not in hiding
I still hear her sing:
"When I am poor black yellow white
A laissez-faire victim, free enterprise failure
Your brother, Sister Ann in squalor."
"When I am wealthy, a privileged graduate
Rockefeller and Rothschild victors
of the system we designed
Our own, American dreams, instant pies,
Self made ones.

She watches her children grow
Hopes for tomorrow,
Cries wars in other lands, Grieves
poor people, inflation, depression,
Famines, Palestinians, Bangla Desh, Oh Israel
Erithrea and Chile.
She'll draw her utopias,
C'est pour demain, ca viendra

But nevermore be humiliated
A trainee at Auschwitz, she mans
hot guns in her deserts
You won't lead her to the slaughter
This time she'll blow you with her.
Hear Nations I am one.

Moshe Yungman
(translated from the Yiddish by Marcia Falk)

THE SACRIFICE

Links of fear
slowly become a chain,
binding my hands and feet.

My father never wanted
to lead me to the sacrifice.
He was bound as I was.
But he led me.

Now I lie on the altar,
my father inside me,
my grandfather inside me.

There is no escape —
no escape.

(UNTITLED)

Don't say I'll have to search farther for
a blade of grass,
a piece of sun.
Don't place me face to face again
with thorns
that men have designed for me.
Don't burn into me again
knives,
eyes,
fear of not being able to raise a hand.
Don't lay me down again
under everyone's feet.
Don't wake me up.

Michael Wyschogrod

SOME THEOLOGICAL REFLECTIONS ON THE HOLOCAUST

The holocaust has been a matter of very great concern to me. I was ten years old when we left Hitler's Berlin in 1939 on our way to the United States. My memories of the Nazi presence are very clear from about the age of five. I remember street fighting between Communists and Nazis in 1933. I remember clearly seeing Hitler on three separate occasions at various public functions. In 1938 my father was deported to Poland together with all Jewish males over the age of 16 who were Polish citizens. I remember the ring of the apartment bell at 6 in the morning, the two Berlin policemen who took my father with them. While they were still in the apartment, my mother told me to leave immediately and notify as many other Jews of Polish citizenship as I could. But it was of no use. Every apartment I visited had already been visited earlier by the police teams. In the afternoon we learned that the collection point for those arrested was a Jewish school not far from where we lived. We quickly made some sandwiches and packed them with some warm sweaters and underwear and took them to the school. Hundreds of Jewish women and children had thought of the same idea and were attempting to get food and clothing to their husbands, fathers and sons. There was a solid line of policemen carrying rifles (usually, Berlin policemen did not carry rifles, of course) surrounding the school. They were not impolite. They simply repeated that the prisoners needed nothing and that medical personnel would travel with them on the way to Poland. These statements were, of course, lies, as we subsequently discovered.

I recount all this—and could go on and on—in order, I suppose, to establish my credentials. On our way to the United States, we spent four weeks in Warsaw in the spring of 1939. I therefore saw

Jewish Warsaw in its last bloom. I shall never forget that experience. From Nazi Berlin, we were thrown into the pulsating Jewish life of Warsaw. We were the refugees from Hitler, the people to be pitied and helped. Warsaw Jewry opened its hearts to these refugees. It was overwhelming. We were on our way to the United States and they were staying, waiting for Hitler to come. They knew it and we knew it. The evening we left Warsaw we hired a horse drawn carriage to transport us and our luggage to the station. On that carriage I wept bitterly and told my mother that I was begging God not to permit the Nazi hordes to lay their hands on these Jews. But God did not listen to me.

Nowadays, rarely does a week go by that I do not read or reread a book about the holocaust. The subject rarely leaves my consciousness. I believe it to be the key to understanding me, should anyone be interested. I may be fooling myself. I may be using the holocaust as a rationalization. My personality may be explainable on quite other grounds than the holocaust. But I do not believe so. And because the holocaust has been so central to me, I have come to some simple conclusions about it which I will now state very simply and briefly. I believe these to be very important conclusions and I wish I could bring them to the attention of every Jew in the world.

1.   The basic message of Judaism is that God is a redeeming God. No proof is needed for this assertion; it is self-evident. It is the basic message of Psalms as it is of the Eighteen Benedictions. There we speak of God as the "shield of Abraham," "who builds Jerusalem," "who gathers the dispersed of Israel," "who heals the sick of Israel," "who resurrects the dead" and so on and so on. All of these are acts of redemption. The basic message of the Eighteen Benedictions is that God is a redeeming God, no matter what and irrespective of how convincing the evidence to the contrary is. Jews have prayed to God "who heals the sick of Israel" after coming home from the funeral of someone loved. They saw that God does not heal all the sick of Israel. Nevertheless, they recited the blessing. The facts had to yield to the proclamation of faith. God was a redeeming God. He heals the sick of Israel. And if it does not seem so, then we just repeat the formula: he heals the sick of Israel. He said he heals them and he does heal them. He will heal them. We can trust him. His promises are not made in vain. They will be fulfilled because he is a

redeeming God.

2.   The holocaust must not be permitted to mute or silence this basic message. It can easily do so. It does so when Judaism is based on the eleventh commandment: thou shalt not hand Hitler a posthumous victory. If I remain a Jew basically to frustrate Hitler's design, I place Hitler's evil design at the heart of Jewish faith. It does not belong there. Only the message that God is a redeeming God belongs there. The holocaust was a totally destructive event. It cannot be made to yield a new lease on life for Judaism.

3.   The holocaust does not enable us to circumvent the question of faith. Jews, of course, are Jews, whether they have faith or not and they remain in the service of God whether they have faith or not. But the holocaust is not a new platform on which all Jews, those with faith and those without it, can unite to preserve Judaism. If I do not believe in the existence of God, either because of the holocaust or independently of it, I have no moral obligation to preserve Judaism because Hitler wished to destroy it. I had a moral obligation to see to it that Hitler was destroyed but once that was accomplished, the desirability of continuing Judaism must be determined by each individual on its own merits. In the absence of faith in the existence of God and the election of the people of Israel, the continuation of the Jewish people can reasonably be construed as a very expensive luxury. If there are many non-believing Jews who are willing to pay this high price, it is not because they are very clear thinkers but because, as Jews, they are in the service of God in spite of their convictions.

4.   It is very dangerous to argue, as Wiesel does, that in connection with the holocaust we are entitled to raise questions but not to provide answers. We either raise a new generation of Jews or we do not. If we do, then we are answering questions as well as raising them. Our answer is an expression of trust in God's promises whether we say so or not or whether we even believe so or not. And as long as that is so, we might as well know what we believe.

5.   The destructive potential of the holocaust should not be underestimated. The holocaust did not cease destroying in May of 1945. When fully faced, it can destroy the faith and even the life of the Jew today. The seriousness of the Richard Rubenstein reaction has been underestimated badly. The holocaust is deeply destructive

of faith and those who continue to believe do so in spite of and certainly not because of the holocaust. I am not persuaded by the argument that the holocaust is just an instance of the ancient problem of evil. That would be true if Judaism were a philosophy dealing with abstract problems. Instead, Judaism is a historic faith which pays very close attention to what happens in history. And the holocaust actually happened. That is the whole point.

6.   I firmly believe that art is not appropriate to the holocaust. Art takes the sting out of suffering. It transforms suffering into a catharsis for which people are willing to pay money to experience. In the final analysis, therefore, art is pleasure even if the raw materials it works with are not. But no such catharsis can be derived from the holocaust. It must remain life and not art. It is therefore forbidden to make fiction of the holocaust. That is why a real writer like Agnon in effect never touched the holocaust. Any attempt to transform the holocaust into art demeans the holocaust and must result in poor art.

7.   The historic memory of the Jewish people has no rivals. The holocaust will therefore be remembered as long as there are Jews. We do not know what the future holds. If there are, God forbid, other holocausts in store for the Jewish people, they, too, will be survived and remembered. But none of them will become the center of Jewish faith. Only acts of redemption can do that. The establishment of the State of Israel is therefore a far more likely prospect to support contemporary Jewish faith than the holocaust. Whatever the future holds—and we pray for the continued prosperity of Israel—it had and has about it the odor of redemption. Right after the Six Day War I cautioned in print against unsubstantiated messianic claims. But it cannot be denied that the odor of redemption is abroad. We have been deceived by such odors before. But one of these times we will not be deceived and it *may* just be this time.

8.   Nothing I have said should be interpreted to mean that I advocate ignoring the holocaust. Our youth should be taught the events as they happened. But, more important, they should be told that the God of Israel is a redeeming God and that the Word of God as spoken by the Prophets of Israel is more certain than the evidence of our senses.

Leonard Levin

WHY THE JEWS?

I am often greatly disturbed by the amount of attention we pay to the Holocaust, an event whose significance seems to be negative on all counts. It is negative in its human aspect—it shows us to what depths of depravity man can sink; it offers us a negative ideal: "Do not be like this, rather be as far removed from this as possible!" It is negative in its theological aspect—if it does not actually shatter our positive ideas of God, it certainly cannot offer them any shred of support. It is negative in its Jewish aspect—far from telling us why we should be proud to be Jews or what positive ideals our Jewishness represents, it shows us Jewishness as a passive identity: to be Jewish means to bear an unendurable stigma, to be the victim par excellence, to have suffered the most monumental persecution in man's history.

At first glance, the most praiseworthy and human response to this seems to be to adopt a universalist stance: Racism, persecution, and intolerance are a plague from which all humanity suffers—learn from this one grand experience of tragedy to oppose discrimination, injustice, and mass murder wherever they occur! Stamp out imperialism, racism, bigotry, prejudice. Liberate all oppressed peoples. Only in a world where there is safety and freedom for all will the Jews be secure.

While I find this attractive in certain respects (as I find the prospect of the coming of the Messiah attractive), I feel it somehow misses the point. After all, it is not the history of *all* racial persecutions to which we are trying to find an adequate response, it is the Holocaust of European Jewry during World War II. The singling out of this one event seems to imply (correctly, in my view) that it was unique in the history of civilized man. And we are back at the same problem: What significance does it have for me, a Jew, that my people were selected from among all the peoples of the world for a unique campaign of hatred and slanderous propaganda extending for the greater part of a century and culminating in the greatest organized mass murder in history? Is there supposed to be something glorious in being victims? Or are we supposed to be martyrs as well? And if so, martyrs for what?

Why, after all, did the Nazis set themselves the task of destroying all the Jews *in the world*? Let us grant that they wanted to purify German culture of its Jewish "corruptions." What did it matter to them whether there were Jews in the Slavic countries, inasmuch as the Slavs were supposedly an inferior people? Why, in fact, if racial contamination was their concern, did they not set out to destroy *all* inferior races? What was their rationale for what they did—what did it mean to them to select the Jews as the one people worthy of supreme infamy and total destruction?

Hitler gave us a clue to this enigma in *Mein Kampf*. Throughout the book, but particularly in the chapter "Nation and Race," we are presented with two diametrically opposed philosophies of life. The one, Hitler's own, is a kind of nature worship combined with social Darwinism and the supremacy of the Aryan race; the other goes by the name of Social Democracy, pacifism, and Judaism, and is opposed to the first in every respect. According to the first philosophy, struggle is the basis of all social existence, both within a single society and between societies. The winner of the struggle is thereby proved to be the best, and fit to rule. Thus:

> A view of life which, by rejecting the democratic mass idea, endeavors to give this world to the best people, that means to the most superior men, has logically to obey the same aristocratic principle also within this people and has to guarantee leadership and highest influence within the respective people to the best heads. With this it does not build upon the idea of the majority, but on that of the personality. (Reynal & Hitchcock edition, 1939, p. 661)

On the other hand:

> The Jewish doctrine of Marxism [i.e., Social Democracy] rejects the aristocratic principle of Nature; instead of the eternal privilege of force and strength, it places the mass of numbers and its

deadweight. Thus it denies the value of the individual in man, disputes the meaning of nationality and race . . . (p. 83f.)

We find a similar dichotomy in Hitler's discussion of the threat of racial cross-breeding:

> To bring about such a development means nothing less than sinning against the will of the Eternal Creator.
> This action, then, is also requited as a sin.
> Man, by trying to resist this iron logic of Nature, becomes entangled in a fight against the principles to which alone he, too, owes his existence as a human being. Thus his attack is bound to lead to his own doom.
> Of course, now comes the typically Jewish, impudent, but just as stupid, objection by the modern pacifist: "Man conquers Nature!"
> Millions mechanically and thoughtlessly repeat this Jewish nonsense, and in the end they imagine that they themselves represent a kind of conqueror of Nature; whereas they have no other weapon at their disposal but an "idea," and such a wretched one at that, so that according to it no world would be conceivable. (p. 392f.)

It is of the utmost importance that we take seriously Hitler's equation of Nature with God, with the consequence that to violate Nature's laws was to commit a sin. The Jews for him were the chief sinners, rebelling against Nature's principles of aristocracy, despotism, racism, and war, and attempting to establish in their place the ideals of human equality, brotherhood, and peace. Hitler's response to this was severe and uncompromising: "Eternal Nature inexorably revenges the transgressions of her laws. Therefore, I believe today that I am acting in the sense of the Almighty Creator: *By warding off the Jews I am fighting for the Lord's work*." (p. 84)

Hermann Rauschning, a former Nazi who defected to the West and tried to impress on Westerners the urgency of defeating Hitler, gave the following account of a conversation with Hitler:

> "But we have been speaking," said Hitler, "of the Jew only as the ruler of the economic world empire. We have been speaking of him as our political opponent. Where does he stand in the deeper struggle for the new world era?"
> I confessed that I had no notion.

"There cannot be two Chosen Peoples. We are God's people. Does not that fully answer the question?"

"That is to be understood symbolically?"

Again he banged the table.

"Symbolically? No! It's the sheer simple undiluted truth. Two worlds face one another—the men of God and the men of Satan! The Jew is the anti-man, the creature of another god. He must have come from another root of the human race. I set the Aryan and the Jew over against each other; and if I call one of them a human being I must call the other something else. The two are as widely separated as man and beast. Not that I would call the Jew a beast. He is much further from the beasts than we Aryans. He is a creature outside nature and alien to nature." (Rauschning, *The Voice of Destruction*, p. 241f.)

This, in my opinion, helps us to set the Holocaust in its proper perspective, as part of the totality of Nazism. Nazism may be regarded, in its broader aspects, as a program to eradicate all Jewish influences from the world—ethical, social, religious—and to enthrone in their place their exact antitheses. In place of an ethic of compassion and justice, an ethic of brutality and conflict was to prevail; in place of an egalitarian social norm, an aristocratic one; in place of a spiritual God, Nature under its darkest aspects was to be worshipped as divine. The physical elimination of the Jews as a people was to be the ritual-symbolic celebration of this transformation of the world, and that is why the destruction of nine million other Europeans had nowhere near the same significance for Hitler as the destruction of six million Jews.

While some may find it cold comfort that the Nazis, while they were killing the Jews, were at the same time paying tribute in an oblique way to the ideals that Jews have lived for, for me it is very important to redeem this supremely tragic episode from the limbo of the absurd. If one must die, it is more bearable to die for a purpose—that may be why even religiously lukewarm Jews sang *ani ma'amin* and *Shma Yisrael* on their way to the gas chambers. Even theologically, the tension is somewhat relieved—the reason God did not rescue the Jews is that it was against God himself that the Nazis declared war, and the Jews, as God's front-line soldiers, were the first to die in the action. (This solution denies God's omnipotence to save his goodness, but has the advantage of addressing the historical realities.)

Even with this understanding, the Holocaust remains absurd, for why should such an enormity of agony be necessary to establish the ethical-religious significance of Judaism which we knew to begin with? Still, I am grateful for this much meaning, for it is only by virtue of this meaning that I dare to offer my defiant affirmation as a challenge to the absurdity that still persists.

Tell ye your children of it, and

Let your children tell their children

And their children another generation

JOEL 1:3

27 NISAN 5735

by Rochelle Saidel Wolk

Bob Salz

TOWARDS A FRAMEWORK FOR TEACHING THE HOLOCAUST

The sensitive nature of the historical phenomenon we call the "Holocaust" makes it very difficult to find an appropriate framework for teaching the subject in our educational institutions. The systematic murder of six million Jews certainly remains emotion-charged for those who survived the concentration camps, and most Jews who were old enough at the time to remember it can still identify with the tremendous catastrophe. Many Jews living outside of Europe who were not directly affected by the killing had relatives and friends who were, and many older American Jews share a feeling of guilt for not being able to help.

However, young Jews who grew up after the Second World War cannot be expected to relate to the Holocaust in the same way as their parents. To them the two great historical traumas of World War II, the Holocaust and the use of the atomic bomb on population centers (even assuming they know something of these events), are not the terrible shocks they were to their parents but are accepted facts of history. They were not personally traumatized by witnessing mass murders and therefore cannot feel them in the highly emotional way their parents do—and many of them can't even understand why their parents get so emotional whenever the subject of the Holocaust comes up. For their part, parents and teachers fail to understand why their children and students do not accept the "self-evident" fact that the Holocaust is relevant to their lives because they are Jewish. Thus one of the greatest impediments to teaching the Holocaust in Jewish schools in America is a communications gap between the generation of teachers and the generation of students.

In the classroom this communications gap manifests itself in the failure of students to understand why they must learn about the Holocaust and in the inability of teachers to explain this to them adequately. Having grown up in North America after the Second World War myself, and having taught about the Holocaust in Jewish schools, I have seen this problem time and time again. As a student, I remember the class asking why we had to learn about all of those terrible things that happened to the Jews in Europe and never receiving an answer that we understood. Instead we were made to feel guilty for not treating the subject with the reverence it deserved. As a teacher, I found that students who are usually excited about studying other subjects groan every time I begin talking about the Holocaust. They absolutely fail to see how these horror stories can possibly be relevant to their lives, and even if they have a grandparent or know of someone who has an Auschwitz number tatooed on his or her arm, they cannot understand how recalling the atrocities can serve any useful purpose to anyone in the present or future. My efforts to explain the reasons to them, which were based largely on what my teachers told me, satisfied neither them or me—but until recently I had nothing else to tell them.

The key to developing a framework for teaching the Holocaust in Jewish schools today, thirty years later, still lies in finding satisfactory answers to the question "Why?". Once we have sufficiently clarified to ourselves why we want to teach the Holocaust and to our students why they should learn about it, the problems of what to teach and how to teach it will also be more easily solved. In order to do this we must first re-evaluate the traditional educational goals which, at least in my experience, have not changed very much in the last thirty years, though the educational needs of the students have.

What are these traditional goals? Which of them should we keep and which should we discard? Some of the aims I have heard most often are:

a) to make sure that succeeding generations of Jews do not forget the victims of the Holocaust.

b) to instill in the students a sense of identity with the Holocaust and thereby strengthen their sense of Jewish identity.

c) to make sure that another Holocaust never happens.

I have no quarrel with the first goal, although I think that it will automatically be achieved once other goals have been realized. It certainly cannot stand alone as a reason for teaching about the Holocaust because students need to know why it is important for them to learn about and remember the victims of the Holocaust today.

The second goal, to instill in the students a sense of identity with the Holocaust and thereby strengthen their sense of Jewish identity, has become the sine qua non of every curriculum or program dealing with the Holocaust I have seen, be it in a Jewish school, a youth group or a summer camp. This goal, so widely shared by Jewish educators, is the major cause of the communications gap between parents and children and between teachers and students. It is based on a number of assumptions with which I must take issue.

First, those who would adopt the instilling of identity as an educational goal must believe that it is possible to instill a sense of identity in a classroom situation. I'm not quite sure what "identifying with the Holocaust" means but it seems that the real aim here, as intended by teachers, youth leaders, et al., is to try to transfer their own emotions to their students. The generation of educators (at least those educators who were already born at the time of the Holocaust) feels sorrow and guilt; sorrow because in the destruction of European Jewry this generation feels a personal loss, and guilt because European Jews were slaughtered while American Jews stood by apparently paralyzed by disbelief and shock.

Somehow, whether consciously or unconsciously, teachers, by "instilling a sense of identity with the Holocaust" are trying to make their students feel what they feel. They assume they can transfer emotions from one generation to another, and this, I believe, is an impossible assumption to make. Emotions are based on experience. Not having lived through those catastrophic years, students in Jewish schools today cannot be expected to see them as most of their teachers do. They do not feel the loss of six million of their people, because they never knew what it was like to have them in the first place. They do not feel guilty for letting the Holocaust happen, because they were not yet alive to prevent it. Not that young Jews should not be expected to relate to the Holocaust at all. The only way they can try to understand it, however, is in the light of their own experience.

This "instilling identity" approach also relies on educational methods that are inappropriate. The best way to evoke emotions is to use gimmickry and ceremony. Who can forget the assemblies with their candle lightings, their moments of silence, and the inevitable filmstrip revealing the gory details of the death camps? These methods undoubtedly produce the desired effect—that of stirring emotions—but do they go beyond it? The evidence of the classroom tells us that they do not. In the classroom students' resentment at being confronted by these emotions outweighs their willingness to discuss them analytically. They do get emotional momentarily but they are loath to engage in any further discussion on what it is they're getting emotional about.

A second dangerous assumption made by the proponents of the "identity" goal is that the Holocaust is an experience which belongs exclusively to the Jews. Many of my teachers used to wallow in the Holocaust, treating it almost as a prized possession not to be shared with a guilt-ridden world. The chief method they used to try to strengthen our Jewish identity was to capitalize on the shock value of the Holocaust. We were told that the Holocaust proved we cannot escape our Jewishness even if we want to. Thus the Holocaust isolated the Jews from the rest of the world even more than ever before. As its victims Jews were considered to be entitled to view the Holocaust as their own catastrophe. Other peoples had no claim to it.

Even apart from dubious value of using the Holocaust to try to create Jewish identity, the assumption that it belongs exclusively to the Jews can only work against the interests of Jewish education. Making this assumption precludes the possibility of non-Jews struggling to come to terms with what happened in the Holocaust. It is true that the Holocaust affects Jews more directly than other people because Jews suffered more than any other people. However, it was also a major event in the history of the modern world. Every child born after the Second World War should in some part of his or her education be confronted by the two great human traumas created by that war—the Holocaust and Hiroshima. The dropping of the atomic bomb on Hiroshima and Nagasaki is not usually treated as an event important only to Japanese history. The far-reaching significance of this event in the history of all humanity is recognized in virtually every social studies textbook used in the public schools.

The scientifically planned murder of six million civilian people in the first organized attempt in recorded history to wipe out an entire "race" is an event of no less importance to the conscience of mankind. As Hannah Arendt points out in *Eichmann in Jerusalem*, Adolf Eichmann was guilty not just of ordinary murder but of crimes against all of humanity. To insist that the Holocaust belongs only to the Jews is to deny the rest of humanity the right to do anything but beat its breast in guilt.

If we look at how the subject of the Holocaust has been treated in public schools, we see that those who would equate the Holocaust with Jewish identity are exacerbating an already bad situation. The public schools and social studies textbooks have so far done their best to avoid dealing with the Holocaust in any great depth. It is usually mentioned (though not always) only briefly as some sort of marginal by-product of the war. The battles of the war and the diplomacy are given much more coverage. When I asked educators why they did not discuss the Holocaust in greater detail most of them told me that they thought it unnecessary to subject young children to such horrible truths. I feel that this is only a partial explanation. Perhaps the more convincing reason is that in non-Jewish schools the Holocaust is not as significant a part of the history of World War II as the battles and the diplomacy. If it were, educators would find it necessary to subject children to the truth, however horrible. For Jewish educators to then treat the Holocaust as an exclusively Jewish tragedy is to justify the lack of attention given to it in the public schools.

The situation in the public schools vis-a-vis the teaching of the Holocaust has consequences in the Jewish schools. Jewish children who attend public schools during the day and Jewish schools in the afternoon hear very little about the Holocaust in the public school—and are then confronted with an emotional approach to it in the Jewish school. Since Jewish children tend to value what they learn in public school above what they learn in Jewish school, many pupils refuse to believe what they learn about the Holocaust in their Jewish school because they did not learn the same things when they covered the topic in public school. I and several of my colleagues have discussed this more than once when we tried to tell the story of the Holocaust to our synagogue school classes. Pupils who studied the Second World War in public school and were told nothing about the Holocaust would absolutely not believe that what I was telling them was true. They would often go back and ask their public school teachers to verify my lessons. It seems to me, therefore, that it is the duty of Jewish educators to enter into dialogue with non-Jewish educators and open the subject of the Holocaust to discussion among teachers and laymen of all faiths. Non-Jewish educators should be encouraged to give the discussion of the Holocaust a more prominent place in their lesson plans. Recent interfaith seminars on the Holocaust, attended by clergymen and academicians have been a positive step in this direction. It is now up to educators to continue the good work.

Now we come to the third traditional goal in teaching the Holocaust, that of making sure it doesn't happen again. The only thing that can be said about this goal is that knowledge of two thousand years of persecution did not prevent the Holocaust itself from happening. Knowledge of pogroms did not prevent further pogroms. Nor has it been proved that those who seem the most determined to prevent another Holocaust, namely those who shout "Never again!" the loudest, know the most about the sources of Holocaust. Knowledge of hate cannot deter hate. The best we can hope for is that our knowledge will induce us to try to create a better world where another Holocaust is unlikely to happen. Looking at today's world, we can hardly say that thirty years of trying to prevent a second Holocaust through education has brought us any closer to creating this better society.

Having evaluated the traditional goals of teaching the Holocaust in Jewish schools, I now feel obligated to offer alternative goals. Most of my reasons for teaching the Holocaust to Jewish children can be found in my criticisms of the traditional educational goals. To me it is important that young Jews learn about the Holocaust:

a)   so that they have knowledge of a most vital part of human history and particularly of their own Jewish history.

b)   so that they are capable of dealing with the many great philosophical, theological and political questions raised by the Holocaust.

c)   so that in their personal relationships and in their political behavior they will work together with non-Jews to create a better world.

As far as the first goal is concerned, besides fulfilling a peculiar human need of knowledge for knowledge's sake alone, knowledge of the Holocaust can serve practical functions as well. It can make young Jews understand why their parents, grandparents and teachers react as they do when the subject of the Holocaust arises, and thus perhaps bring the different generations closer together. But in order to do this we must teach the subject in a rational manner. Instead of saying to the students, "You must learn about the Holocaust because you must feel these and these emotions," the teacher should say, "You should learn this material because it covers a very important event in history" or "because your parents lived through this event and they feel these and these emotions that you should try to understand."

Another practical use for knowledge of the Holocaust is for young Jews to be able to discuss the matter intelligently with their non-Jewish friends and to perhaps fill the gap in their education. I once taught the Holocaust in a New York City public high school social studies class. As I was describing the death camps and the gas chambers, a few Black students in the class began to cheer. When I asked them why they were cheering, they explained that the Jews got what they deserved because they were the ones who owned the plantations in the south and made slaves of the Blacks. At this point I noticed that the Jewish students in the class were frustrated and bewildered because they didn't know enough about the subject to say anything. Some of them even agreed that the Jews must have been guilty of something for receiving such a terrible punishment. A little knowledge would have gone a long way here.

I proposed my second goal because I feel that it is necessary for all people to deal with the great moral questions of the day. The Holocaust raises myriad questions about the existence of God, God's justice, His relationship to the Jewish people, the nature of Man, the justification for the creation of the State of Israel and so on. These are questions onto which a Jewish child may stumble along the path of his or her moral development.

The third goal, that of working together with non-Jews to create a better world, is a dream. However, if we learn anything from the bitter experience of the Holocaust, we learn that we must teach our children to change the world. The Holocaust has terribly offended humanity. It is a permanent stain on the collective conscience of mankind—an extreme example of the depths of depravity to which human beings can sink. As long as children are taught about the Holocaust, they will have before them this horrifying example of where the world can go if they let it. This reason for teaching the Holocaust may sound like—but is not exactly the same as—the traditional one of "making sure that it never happens again." Whereas the latter implies an aggressive stance, that of always being on the alert and being prepared to react physically to any perceived threat, the former calls for moral change. In order to effect this moral change, each Jewish child must first strive for a high level of personal moral development in his or her relationships with other people and must then work politically to oppose all forms of tyranny and oppression with which he or she comes in contact. The traditional goal implies a defensive withdrawal on the part of Jews while the aim I propose calls for a reaching out to all people in an effort to work together to realize the dream that grew out of the nightmare.

If we move for a moment from what *we* want for ourselves and for our children in teaching the Holocaust and look at *their* needs, we will see that the outward-directed educational goals are more compatible with the needs of students than the traditional ones. Jewish children in America today generally relate to the society as a whole more than to the Jewish world. They have non-Jewish friends, they go to non-Jewish schools for a longer time than they go to Jewish schools, they watch non-Jewish television programs and see non-Jewish movies. To teach them about the Holocaust on a basis that asks them to withdraw into a shell and mistrust the non-Jewish world which makes up the greater part of their daily experience is to ask them to do something they cannot do. It is no wonder that Jewish children are so uncomfortable with the subject of the Holocaust and resent it so much. The proponents of the traditional goals will argue that the Holocaust teaches us that Jews will never be able to feel secure among non-Jews—that anti-Semitism will always be with us. They may be right, but if this means that Jews and Gentiles cannot discuss the Holocaust in a common forum and cannot, having learned its lessons, strive together to create a better world, then there is no hope for the Jews, or for the world.

lyn lifshin

1944

sometimes there was chocolate

in radio stories there
were always tunnels
with germans in them

even the children dreamed
what they'd do to
young girls

there were no fathers

lyn lifshin

1945

mallets bay the
3rd cottage in
the circle june
the smell of oil
cloth linoleum
smoke the girl

who sat told us
there was smoke
from the bodies
in that tunnel
poland she said
you could smell
the hair i didn't

want to remember
ate choclate
brushed ants
from a doll
stuffed in a
shoe box near
the bed i tried

thinking of the
girl in the
roller skating
rink one eye
green one blue
flecked with
yellow but

what they did
to children
came thru the
leaves was in
the beacon from
the lighthouse

Yossi Klein

PLEA

1.

If there be 50 righteous men in Auschwitz,
who walked to the mountain to pray every Sabbath,
hand in hand with little Isaac,
body thin as side-curls,
raised as a Jew to be sheared—
Send the ram back to the forest.
Only grant Abraham the shoichet's blade,
whose soft breath is merciful death.

2.

If there be 40 women of virtue in Auschwitz,
daughters of Israel, violated Sabbath Queens
     cringing in their nakedness—
Let holiday skirts cover char-greyed skin,
let their modesty stifle death's twisted passions.

3.

If there be 30 elderly innocents in Auschwitz,
whose only sin is of a dying tree,
What harm to forgo the final indignity?
Calm the wind—
Let them fall as they had grown,
unheard, unnoticed, gently humming
     out of the earth.
And bring soft beds into the ovens,
and family portraits to beckon them to stillness.

4.
If there be 20 blameless invalids in Auschwitz,
bent smokestacks coughing out
    life that once was—
Tell the doctors not to please mock like schoolboys,
and with the reverence of science
    for a colony of germs
solemnly dissect the jerking bodies
no one else had any use for at all.

5.
If there be 10 children in Auschwitz.
A single fetus clinging to the womb.
Your laughter, Sarah: don't stop it.
Don't stop it, Sarah,
don't stop it—
Summon God's angels from the watchtowers,
and return their gift of little bones,
You are much too old to have a son.

Barry Ivker

A JEW IN LOVE

I came in the name of
love, the arch-
bishop said at his
trial—in the name of
freedom for all man-
kind—in the name of—
Jesus.
I have heard of that kind of
love before—agape they
call it—the love of all
mankind.
And we have been em-
braced before—by all
mankind—lick-
ed by the sen-
suous tongues of Span-
ish flames in the
name of love, bear-
hugged by Rus-
sian peasants on Ea-
ster Sunday in the name of—
Jesus.
We have heard the
beckoning call of those
anxious for our sal-
vation, of miss-
ionaries sent to Brigh-
ton Beach to woo the
remnants of the camps in
their own tongue.

And it has come to this—
That in a gathering of my
gentile friends, the barest
mention of good will to
all mankind finds me
standing with my mouth
agape.
The prelate spoke of
love—as they re-
moved the grenades from his
cartrunk he spoke pas-
sionately of his
love.
And his nuns cried when
they heard the sentence—
twelve years of kosher
food for this man of
peace—compliments of the
sovereign state of Is-
rael.
Should the thought of
such parochial fare
gag this lover of
mankind, I would be
ready to send a philtre of
my own devising—to ease his
swallowing—a token
gift—for a univer-
salist—from a Jew in
love.

Bob Rosenbloom

ss man

reichkind, wunderkind,
son of light, son of bitch,
distillation of aryan greatness,
the einsatz have tasted this wine,
i, french hotel owner,
throw the bottle away in a trash heap,
a pyramid of broken bottles.
nietzsche, schopenhauer,
wagner and himmler,
i hope these stars fade
in the night.
i excuse art and the art of murder.
what if j were king?
germany drunk on light,
moonshine of nazi rhetoric,
son of fire, fag, pimp
whore of hell.
i thought you were great.
you are a civil service storm trooper.
knock, knock. get out jew.
you will die
for not returning your library book.
german odds, armored tanks
versus starving jews.
five aces but you bet one mark and call.
was it status to turn on the gas jets?
the girl asked what you did.
i gun down sheep, shoot fish in a barrel.

don't ask. it pays.
i forgive pigs, not humans.
from thirty-seven to forty-four
you were not inhuman.
honey, i bully ghetto jews.
are you impressed?
will you marry me?
the band of gold is a ring of fire.
why won't your finger fall off?

B. Z. Niditch

For Nelly Sachs
(IN MEMORIAM)

CHRYSTAL NIGHT

In the black forest
resting below yellow stars
Sabbath Eve wails her sirens
toward the raven sky

Hovering by smokestacks
a dozen oven birds
warm limbs of birches
on a parchment tree

Tablets old as Germany
are torn from holy arcs
as desolate gravediggers howl
their prophetic parables

Is this the time, we ask
of Jacob's troubles—
rising from Satan's
bloodstock cities?

As the remnant of glass
swept in the snow
by the synagogue
over a soldiers dirt boot

Where is the dove
transfixed to an olive branch
facing her Adam's rib
in the skeleton sunlight.

B. Z. Niditch

OSWEICIM

In rows crossing a votive stone
shoes were inlaid among dusters
Sandals of winter stars
and the prophets' beards
we brushed aside
for the ghost riders
calling her morning's requiem,
Here your warm eyesores singed
amid the steppes and minefields
of your Fathers,
"Am I an outsider?"
"Rather, am I worthy to live,"
We paused among barbed wire
raven upon oven birds
swept in the hollow of our hands
we held as stoneflowers together
"Are you my bride?"
"Rather, Are you my children:"
When nightmares yellowing stargazers
and tomorrow's sudden rainmaker
hoists her All-Souls forecast
arcangels shall walk here
shoe upon shoe (engraved only to God)
on the snows of Poland.

Beth Broder Epstein

MEETING IN TEL AVIV

The day we had entered was a Germanic or Slavic gray, not what we had expected. Rain flooded the streets of Tel Aviv: the city is unprepared for such torrents, but the winter needed this rain. Now the city seemed as unready for the downpour as it was to absorb the people who had come home to it. Such largess is not to be counted on, so, for the time being old women waded ankle-deep into the streets, while traffic forced its way downtown, shooting whirlpools it created and soaking the walkers. The young professionals rushing to their jobs and appointments seemed not to notice.

We would have been better off, if we could have planned it, to postpone our first meeting with Uncle Asher. Really, he is no uncle at all. He is the second or perhaps the third husband of my grandmother's sister Rachel. I say second or third, because in the years after my grandparents died, no one spoke Yiddish to me and I came to this meeting rusty and sophomoric. I don't know if Asher told me that Rachel had two houses before the war or two husbands. I don't say anything about my grammar: at best I managed appropriate signs and nods to his story. I could have said very little, but Asher rarely paused in his telling, as he might have done if he needed me to speak. In any case, Aunt Rachel had lost either or both before the end of the war, before she met Asher in Israel.

The family's story, the one I had grown up with, was that when the Germans came, she and her husband were sent to different camps. Each was told the other was dead, so this first or second husband remarried and fathered a child in the camp. When it was over, and Rachel remet her husband, she told him to go with the mother of his child. She hadn't any to keep him. This story had never satisfied me because I could not understand how conditions in a camp allowed for marriage and birth. And were communications so normal as to inform about the life or death of inmates at other camps? Why would people credit these communications? I would rather not believe this story: I see wedding canopies fashioned from barbed wire and honeymoon cottages with wall-to-wall marriage cots. How could a woman conceive life in a concentration camp? Was it so bad, ever, if a child could be born? On the other hand, this is the fleshing out of the macabre, and out of six million stories, it is plausible this did happen and in just this manner. The husband's bigamy makes a truce between illusion and reality: what a wedding it must have been for him. And it was no accident that could take a living husband from my aunt when so many other husbands were taken dead. By now, we all know that there is no such thing as an accident, and no place left for a child to be born under a bad star, or a good one for that matter.

But there is another issue here. Although I try, I cannot remember when I heard this story. I cannot remember who told it to me, or what I was doing when I heard it. I suppose it must have been my mother; grandparents never speak to children of such things. On the other hand, it is just possible that I myself produced the story of Rachel's past, or, given some kernel, cultivated it into its present form. Definitely, I would not wish to discuss the issue with my mother. I have known the story so long that, after all, it is mine.

The first time we had met Aunt Rachel, the day was as it should be, almost tropical. We had taken a car from the kibbutz where we were staying as supervisors to a group of college students; then a bus in Tel Aviv to the social worker's office on Rechov Mikve Israel. The street contrived to look like a Mediterranean east Bronx: the office itself seemed in need of a dole. It was the social worker's day off, but we managed the conversation with the concierge well enough to get the name of the hospital where Rachel is staying. I call him a concierge, though just as easily he could have been the "shames" of the establishment, or one of the more experienced office cases, now become a professional overseer. He seemed to know the ropes pretty well. Following his directions, to get to Bat Yam we forced our way onto two more spicy, dark buses by what was obviously the most indirect route.

Beit Holim is part of a large complex of hospital wards, modern, clean and discreetly landscaped. There are luxurious plants clinging to the surrounding fences. The patients, all wearing the same green pajama costumes, sun themselves within the gates of the compound. The building where Rachel stays is in the center of the complex and it is different: the structure is made of sterile, grey cement components, as if to erect its own shade. No patients from Beit Holim sun themselves. These are no mere losers: born dead, they have been yellowed by no ordinary sun.

The ward where she sits is equipped with an inner window giving out onto the corridor, so that the attendants do not have to go inside to see the patients. In the middle of the inner window I saw her. It is impossible to say how old Aunt Rachel is. Each woman has her secrets; Asher says he does not know, and there is no one else to tell. I saw the family resemblance, the deep-set "bedroom eyes" of certain proudly lascivious cousins, the wide, unlined forehead of my grandmother and mother, the big women of the family. The rest had been rushed away, or it had sunk inside the structure and been stifled by the dry husk. Miraculously, the fingernails still seemed to grow. Otherwise, Rachel was her own tomb. She was a naked woman clothed in certain stories.

The eyes were useless because of cataracts, so she used her hands. Someone, probably one of the other inmates, had painted her fingernails a soft rose sometime back: it was a hideous joke out of the past. She reached out for my hand when I came toward her. The attendant locked the door behind us, but it seemed unnecessary; everyone inside was very quiet.

I remembered being told that when the other girls had been sent away to America, Rachel had been the one doted on, the real beauty of all the Kerner daughters. She was the youngest, the cultured and wealthy one who had stayed behind on the family estate in Rumania—I know they grew apples—and she had become an only child.

The nurses had taken away her false teeth, fearing she might choke on them, so I had difficulty listening to her. Rachel first tried Hebrew with me, then what seemed like Russian, then something else I could not understand, questioning me with potent facility, indulgently trying out languages I would understand, finally settling into a polished Yiddish I hadn't heard in years. She seemed to understand when I told her I was a relative, and she began to listen with a quiet hunger. She was like a lady enduring the blessings over a meal that was to break her long fast. It was the eve of the Day of Atonement.

Then, the eyes focused and the lady began daintily to "davin," rocking, leaning back and forth in her plastic chair, whispering certain prayers. That is, it was a dry, awkward swaying rather than the rocking one does of a child, though perhaps one does this with a dead child.

To her, I was my mother, Esther. Her face went exuberant and wet, into the past. She told me that she had received letters from her American sisters:

YOU HAVE A NEW NIECE . . . A NEW GRANDNIECE. WE ARE ALL HEALTHY HERE.

In her clear minute, she told me I was her beautiful, good niece, a fine child from her good sister. "From Miriam?"

Then she fumbled for the hand of the woman sitting next to her, and put that hand into mine, both by way of introduction and termination. The face composed itself. With the versatility of the almost dead, her hands touched her pajamas here and there, checked buttons, and rested away from me in her lap. This merciful resourcefulness is to be respected.

I had come expecting to make things right for her, to bring her gifts and pictures of the family, and to fix what could not be fixed. I could not have known such delicacy existed; what traveling she had done to console me!

With Asher it is different. He had been waiting for us since May, when my mother had written that her daughter and son-in-law would arrive in January. And he had been waiting for us at the social worker's office to discuss where Rachel was to be placed permanently. The rain had some time ago seeped through his coat and beneath his Russian-style lamb's wool hat. Smelling of mildew, he rose to meet us, kissing both our hands. This is, perhaps, some custom out of the Polish shtetl. Or it is his own old-man's innocent pantomime, so impromptu that it blesses and curses at once. The ritual comforted me. It was like seeing for the first time a map of the Bronx neighborhood where I had grown up. The names of the familiar streets were printed officially in red or black, names I had forgotten because I knew them too well.

He had been very tall; now he is pulled over taut. His hands look like a mason's, but I had heard he was a women's tailor. The blue pin-striped suit he wears hangs away from him. Had it ever been his?

The two social workers begin:

"Ah, the two 'famous relatives' from America. We have been waiting for you. You see, Rachel needs a guardian in Israel, someone to look out for her interests and affairs. We are afraid that Asher is incompetent. Maybe he is senile himself, or he wants her wealth for his old age. It's not inconceivable, after his own experiences and sense of insecurity. Anyway, Rachel cannot stay in Bat Yam, which is for curable patients. She is mostly vacant, incontinent, and these people need special care in private rest homes that cost money, after all. Of course, the municipality has offered to pay something towards her support, but Asher doesn't like the idea. But these places are very nice, considering how miserable these places are in America. These are not worse, considering who wants to be hired to clean up. . . . "

"Rachel gets a pension from the government and Bonn pays her something. Germany made a big settlement with her a few years ago: ten thousand."

"And we think Asher wants to keep this money. He has become very independent. He won't sign the papers to commit her, but now that the 'famous relatives' have arrived, he must be persuaded to make the decision. Help him to understand. She won't get better. Bat Yam needs the space."

I mention that my family heard she had scrubbed floors in Israel, and had sent her money. There is no legal proof that Germany "settled" with her, only gossip from neighbors in the refugee apartments where she had lived with Asher. I tell them what they already know: she has no relatives in Israel, and only distant ones in America, to whom Rachel is a name from a childhood story.

The social workers tell me that Rachel and Asher lived behind a locked door, that their apartment smelled like a warehouse, it was filled with refuse, that she could do no worse in an American home for the aged. "But Asher doesn't like these places. He refuses to commit her, he stalls. These places do not have many openings. You can't be sure these places will accept her in her condition. . . . "

Their mistakes become less and less indignities. "But that is your responsibility, your job. You are supposed to know where there are openings. What do you mean, 'in her condition'? These places are for her kind, you said."

All this is in English, and Asher does not understand it. He looks at us with damp boy's eyes and raises his chin. "What are you saying? Here, look."

He has been waiting a long time for this. The conversation goes on around us. His Yiddish has lifted me out of that. He has pictures, cracked and frayed around the edges, brown-tinted, stylized portraits of two staring babies.

"Look. My babies." He makes a gesture with his index finger, circling his throat. "Hitler. My wife . . . " Again the circle around the throat, then the palm of his hand opens half-way and the shoulders go up and inward and finally the chin lifts. Another picture surfaces. Asher shuffles it under the pile quickly, as if it were a joker. It is nobody I know, a smiling old man standing next to a cart, holding a book open, eyes averted.

"More pictures. Look." Rachel, younger, in a white blouse, lounging on a rock with ankles crossed, somewhere in Israel. She is smiling straight into the camera. "My bride, a good woman sent from God. Writes and reads all kinds of languages, but she speaks even more," he tells me in Yiddish, slowly, so that I can understand.

"More pictures": of a young couple in leather hiking shorts, climbing a mountain, eyes focused on the camera. "My bride, me. My two boys." Again the gesture beginning with the index finger. "Hitler." It seems that the word intends to frame the beginning of a sentence that would not, after all, be complete. The pictures are the ends of stories.

The conference is over. Asher has a list of rest homes to inspect. They are all bad, they are all the best there are, they are all unacceptable, he must be made to accept. The social workers thank us for something.

We take a bus with Asher to visit Aunt Rachel again. It is late, and we are a little concerned about the buses running to the kibbutz on a Friday afternoon. Furthermore, Asher insists on paying our fares. He tells us money doesn't matter. "Your health comes first."

The bus is crowded and we must sit separated. The rain has stopped, so the clouds make the shadows instead. Asher is excited: he shouts that Israel is a good land, better than America where there are Communists. "After Hitler, the Communists, but to live in Israel is something else. All the children live in America. Rachel always cries for the children, Miriam's children." He repeats this so that we can understand.

Out of the bus, he moves like an impatient convalescent unsure of his legs, his size and strength surprising him, repeating his story to make sure we understand. I am giddy from my race with the old man, who is rushing us to Beit Holim by a short-cut, and from my race into the past for a vocabulary. We hurry through an empty lot next to the hospital where there are signs, even in English, saying "Passage Prohibited," and "Quiet." I am angry at the past: no one had bothered to teach me to speak Yiddish, only to understand it. Now that time responds with silence, and there is nothing I can say, and no accusations I can make towards my own defense. There are no criminals in my past, only victims.

We are all together: Rachel, Asher, my husband and I and the still muttering women in the sitting room, this side of the observation window. Today she does not know me, and I wonder if I imagined that she did the first time we met. I think that, today, Asher is for Rachel her father. He brings out a package of food I had not noticed. He feeds her a soft yellow apple that miraculously is not rotten inside. It is so ripe and soggy that she can eat it without her teeth, sucking up the juice from around her chin, a child enjoying her father's treat. Then, thick red jelly oozing everywhere, a whole filled donut. He uses his handkerchief to catch the crumbs. Her hunger amazes me.

He tells her I am here, and she cries exuberantly for him—for Asher or for her father—for the one who feeds her, not for me. Aimlessly, her hand pats my cheek because I am here. Asher understands and apologizes: "Hitler, the cataracts, an accident and a fall two years ago, and her lunch must be late today."

After Rachel has eaten, we suggest taking Asher to a restaurant in Tel Aviv. He thinks that he will be treating us, so he agrees. We suggest each restaurant that we pass, but he says no to all of them. He eats only Kosher food, but we have forgotten.

He leads us to a tiny luncheonette, also smelling of mildew, where Asher orders one course at a time, showing us how not to betray him by hurrying, discussing each choice with the waiter who speaks good Yiddish. We keep thinking he has finished eating, and my husband goes up to the counter, trying to pay the bill so that Asher will not have to use his own money, and so that we can leave graciously and in time to catch our last bus before Shabbat.

Again it is raining, and Asher, crying, tells the waiters and the few last diners that I am his sick wife's relative from America. I smile tensely and nod to them all, thinking about the time. What had been a light, free-floating headache has become a systematic landing of tiny weights behind my eyes, so I tell him that we will see him again in Tel Aviv before we return home, but we cannot say exactly when: we must be with our students. We will let him know when to expect us. He has no telephone: we will write to him. He shakes his head to respond, and he stumbles out of the restaurant into the thick, wet crowd rushing to get home to Shabbat.

William B. Helmreich

HOW JEWISH STUDENTS VIEW THE HOLOCAUST
A Preliminary Appraisal

Despite the recent tremendous upsurge of interest within the Jewish community as a whole concerning the Holocaust, we have virtually no empirical evidence on how Jews perceive what was perhaps the most cataclysmic event in Jewish history. We do not know how Jews view the Germany of today, what they think of European Jewry's response to the Holocaust, nor whether they feel a repetition of such events is a possibility in the United States.

To begin looking seriously at this painful yet crucial topic, a preliminary study was undertaken in 1973. In-depth interviews were conducted by trained college students with 42 undergraduates at various institutions in New York State and in Connecticut.** The interviewers were each asked to interview three students whom they knew previously and with whom they felt considerable rapport. Those interviewed were students at various institutions including the City College of New York, Yale University, Adelphi University, and Brooklyn College and ranged in age from 17 to 22. Significantly, almost all had had some formal Jewish education, including quite a few who had gone to Yeshiva high schools. The questions were designed to open up the discussion to a broader consideration of the different aspects of the Holocaust. Although I have made some tabulations, this was a relatively small sample. The primary purpose of the study was to understand the range of possible and probable responses. In other words, my goal here was quality, not primarily quantity.

While many in the Jewish community have emphasized the need

**The author wishes to thank the students in his seminar at Yale University and those in his course at the City College of New York who conducted the interviews for this study.

to increase the understanding of today's generation about the Holocaust, the interviews indicated that students were already somewhat knowledgeable and certainly quite interested in this subject. When asked whether they had ever read anything on the Holocaust more than 80% replied that they had. Taking into consideration the possibility that some students may have felt a bit embarrassed at appearing uninformed on this subject, the interviewers probed further and discovered that almost three-quarters of this group claimed to have read not one, but several books on the Holocaust. When pressed as to what these were the students cited various books. The works of Elie Wiesel and Arthur Morse's book, *While Six Million Died*, were among those mentioned most often. It did not appear from the interviews as though the students were obtaining their information primarily from college programs or courses in this area but rather as a result of their own reading. In addition, students did not, for the most part, perceive the Holocaust as an event remote from their own lives. In fact, almost two-thirds were acquainted with someone who had lived through the Holocaust, in many instances a relative.

One of the questions raised in the interviews was the attitude of the students toward Germany today. Respondents were asked whether they would ever consider visiting Germany. By a 57% to 36% margin, those responding indicated that they would consider such a visit. Seven per cent were undecided. While some of the answers indicated that the respondents had not given much thought to the question, a good number gave detailed replies that indicated a considerable degree of ambivalence. Typical was the following exchange between the interviewer and a 20-year-old junior at City College:

Int. Would you ever consider visiting Germany?

Res. I guess I would consider it. I suppose I might consider it.

Int. Why?

Res. Well, just because awful things happened there doesn't necessarily mean you have to stay away. I know it would probably give me an eerie feeling to be there since so many tragedies have happened in my family because of what went on there; but, you know . . . , it's like blaming me for something that happened in a war that I wasn't responsible for. That's the same thing like blaming a German 19-year-old for what happened. It just seems to me to be a little silly to do that. I could understand how my parents would do that, but I'm of a different generation.

Another student, a junior at Yale, expressed his uncertainty in the following manner:

Int.   What is your impression of Germany today in light of what happened to the Jews?

Res.   I think for that to have occurred, you can't dismiss it. Well, there was a depression. There was a strong leader with some fancy rhetoric. There was something in those people just as there was in people all over. It could happen here although it might not be that easy here. I dislike the people. I'm suspicious of them. Any group willing to blindly follow a leader and his ideals are not your normal kind of people, certainly to be watched.

Int.   Would you ever visit Germany?

Res.   Yes. I'm curious. I hear it's a beautiful country. I think I'd go over with a chip on my shoulder. I'd get into an argument. I'd want to see the concentration camps and picture in my mind what occurred there. I don't feel any desire, however, to see "beautiful Germany" with its gorgeous castles and Rhine River. I would see it and be impressed, but to me it's still "Deutschland."

On the other hand, those who felt no inclination to visit Germany were not ambivalent at all. Their positions were stated clearly and unequivocally: "No, I would not. I dislike the German people."; "I would never think of visiting it because of the Holocaust."; or, "I would never set foot in that country." Interestingly, further probing indicated that for many students their reason for not wanting to set foot in Germany was not really based on a hatred of the German people per se but rather on the unhappy thoughts and memories that such a trip would provoke. The comments made by a Queens College sophomore on this subject are revealing:

Int.   Would you ever consider visiting Germany?

Res.   No.

Int.   Why not?

Res.   It would be very oppressive and I wouldn't enjoy myself.

Int.   Wouldn't you want to at least experience it?

Res.   It would simply depress me.

Students were also asked to comment on the behavior of European Jews directly before and during the Holocaust itself. In general, students felt that the Jews failed to recognize the precariousness of their situation until it was too late, (although they could not be blamed for doing so). The question of the Jewish response *during* the Holocaust, however, received a very different reaction. A wide range of views were expressed—many of which were condemnatory, some of which were laudatory, and a few of which merely revealed the ignorance of the respondents. Nearly half expressed strong criticism of Jews, referring to them as cowards, fools, or worse. Some examples follow:

> How did the Jews let themselves be led to the camps? Why didn't they fight back? If I was going to a camp I think I would have fought back and refused to go. —*a 20-year-old junior at CCNY.*

> The Jews just sort of accepted it and went off to the concentration camps like sheep. —*an 18-year-old freshman at Yale.*

> They didn't even attempt to unify themselves and speak to the world, having been persecuted for so long. —*a 19-year-old sophomore at Brooklyn College.*

> Why didn't they fight? Some did, but not enough. No one really had the courage to stand up. Not even the American Jews. —*a 19-year-old sophomore at Brooklyn College.*

> European Jews made the mistake of believing so strongly in their religion that they could not see beyond it. And so they behaved like a bunch of _____ —*a 20-year-old senior at Yale.*

Clearly these comments reflect a good deal of bitterness and hostility, not to mention a lack of understanding concerning the Jews' actual ability to resist. This is particularly disturbing when one considers that the overwhelming majority of those who felt European Jews were cowards professed to have read more than one book on the Holocaust and that the books mentioned often dealt with this issue.

There were other responses given to this question that indicated a view that in fact Jews were powerless to affect their own fate (about 25% of those answering) although even this was often combined with some criticism. One student, a junior at Yale, said:

> I think for that to have occurred European Jewry must have been blind to some extent. Once they were locked into the concentration camps there wasn't a whole lot they could do. But you get a feeling that they were passive, an attitude which I wouldn't have adopted. But then again, you don't know the conditions. I try to identify more with a Warsaw uprising and a fight rather than being herded into a car and saying: "Everything's all right." The idea of the state gathering me and my family up! I'd shoot them first!

The last comment, which appeared in many interviews, underscores the need to make today's generation more aware of how the will to resist was slowly and systematically destroyed by the Nazis. It is also significant that only three students in the entire sample mentioned resistance on the part of European Jewry. Also surprising was the relatively high proportion of respondents who were not sure how they felt about the entire issue. Close to one-fourth of those answering were unable to formulate any opinion at all. Obviously, such a "don't know" response may signify either ambivalence or ignorance.

There were, in addition, several unusual responses on this subject. One student felt that the Holocaust had the important effect of unifying the Jews. Another student, a sophomore at Yale who described herself as a pacifist declared:

> I think that there is a belief that the Jews should not have allowed themselves to be led to the slaughter and that they should have taken up arms and used Nazi tactics, an attitude which I find abhorrent. I think there was something beautiful in the way they went.

Another issue that drew a number of interesting responses was the question of how the Holocaust affected the way in which the world viewed the Jews. Almost two-thirds of those interviewed believed that the world felt sympathy and guilt, although a good number emphasized that this was only a temporary phenomenon.

> The world may have felt some degree of sympathy toward the Jews

but I think their overall view did not change. —*an 18-year-old freshman at City College.*

The world once more pitied the Jewish people. The image of the Jew continued to be that of a weakling but the image of the Holocaust terrifed the world and made it feel guilty. —*a 19-year-old sophomore at City College.*

The world has felt very guilty because without much effort quite a few Jews could easily have been saved. Anyway I think the world turned its back on the Palestinian refugees after 1948 because it felt guilty. And I think the effects of the Holocaust kept the world from condemning Israel until 1967. But ever since then this feeling of guilt has been eliminated by the military successes of Israel. Therefore, I think the effects have worn off and things are going to get worse. —*a 22-year-old senior at Yale.*

Generally speaking, almost no one seemed to feel that the Holocaust had resulted in a fundamental change in the non-Jews' perception of the Jew. In fact a substantial number of persons stated that while there may have been some sympathy for the Jews after the war the world had actually learned very little or nothing from the Holocaust. An 18-year-old sophomore at Brooklyn College observed:

The world basically couldn't care less because it didn't involve them. If it did scare them, it did so only because it threatened democracy as a whole. They took no pity on the Jews themselves.

The general tone that emerges from the responses is a cynical one. However, more than a quarter of those responding indicated that the establishment of the State of Israel could be cited as a positive development whose origins lay in the Holocaust.

The plight of Soviet Jewry has received a great deal of attention in the past few years from a wide spectrum of groups within the American Jewish community. Many young Jews have been very active in this area. Thus it was not surprising that the overwhelming majority, almost 90% of those queried, answered "yes" when asked if the situation of Soviet Jewry was one with which Jews throughout the world ought to concern themselves. Most cited the responsibility of one Jew towards another as their reason, although some also placed their statements within a larger framework of concern for the human rights of all people to live in freedom.

When asked if the predicament of Soviet Jewry was at all analogous to that faced by the Jews in the Nazi era, more than 60% said it was not because it was necessary to distinguish between physical and spiritual oppression. Most perceived the major problem in the Soviet Union as one involving freedom of religion. Despite the publicity given the emigration problem (even as early as 1973) hardly any students identified the denial of emigration rights as a primary form of anti-Jewish persecution.

Those who regarded the situation as analogous seem to consider spiritual persecution as serious a violation of human rights as physical oppression. However, neither they nor any other students talked about the violence to which many Soviet Jews are subjected. Not a single student mentioned the lengthy prison terms or the executions that are the fate of some Soviet Jews. No mention was made of Jews who are beaten and cowed into submission when they apply for exit visas. Yet, as I have noted, despite this tendency to underestimate the seriousness of the conditions under which Soviet Jews live, the overwhelming majority *still believed* that Jews everywhere had the obligation to help Russian Jewry. In other words, the right to worship and otherwise identify as Jews was considered an issue of primary importance.

The attitudes of students toward the Holocaust can best be analyzed if it is discussed in terms of how secure these students feel about being Jewish in today's world. Such a comparison would also tell us something about the possible long-range effects of the Holocaust.

Students were asked whether they felt there was much or little anti-Semitism in the United States today. More than two-thirds felt there was a great deal of anti-Jewish feeling throughout the country. The responses pointed to a rather high level of concern, insecurity, and even anxiety concerning the existence of anti-Semitism. Interestingly, student after student took care to emphasize that anti-Semitism was present primarily in "other" regions of the United States, not in the urban Northeast. Moreover, most respondents stressed that the anti-Semitism that did exist was of a very subtle nature, a factor that may have made it appear all the more insidious to some. The examples that follow reflect the prevalence of both these views:

> Yes there is a good deal of anti-Semitism. It's very easy growing up in an East Coast intellectual environment to think that the world is Jewish, that the whole world loves Jews. I am suspicious of that notion. —*a 21-year-old junior at Yale.*

> Anti-Semitism is prevalent in different forms. If you are in the South or Midwest you are marked just for being a Jew. Nothing can be done about this view because it's a matter of life-long conditioning. —*a 19-year-old sophomore at Brooklyn College.*

> It [anti-Semitism] exists pretty strongly but it is very subtle. It's starting to come out a lot more now because of the oil situation. My roommate told me a story about her boyfriend's brother-in-law who is a professor out West and who will take two identical papers and if one belongs to a Jewish student he will deliberately subtract points because of the feelings out there concerning competition with Jews. —*an 18-year-old freshman at the State University of New York, Oneonta.*

While the individual above clearly relied upon fourth-hand information to support her point of view, this was not always, or even usually, the case:

> I know there are a hell of a lot of anti-Semites but not in the big cities. In every Midwestern town there are anti-Semites. It's not because they hate the Jews. It's just that they hate something they can't understand. In one small town I met this kid about my age. We became friendly. A few days later he found out I was a Jew and he said: "You must have Catholic blood in you because you sure don't act like a Jew." I said to him: "You must have some Jewish blood in you because you don't act like a Catholic." That was the last time either of us made a reference to religion. In a couple of towns I decided not to spend the night because of the hostility toward Jews. I could go on for days. —*a 20-year-old junior at Brooklyn College.*

When asked if they themselves had experienced anti-Semitism 54% replied yes. Over two-thirds of those who believed there was considerable anti-Semitism in the United States asserted that they had been victims of such prejudice. Of even greater significance is that almost one-third of those questioned who believed the amount of anti-Semitism in the United States to be substantial could *not* recall any such encounters in their own lives.

Those respondents who asserted that they had been victimized by anti-Semitism were asked to describe their experiences. Virtually all of these turned out to be verbal as opposed to physical encounters. A Brooklyn College coed recounted the following experience:

> I once went away with my parents to a Pennsylvania resort area where we were the only Jewish people. While staying with some of the kids there, they made some nasty remarks about Jews and I realized how anti-Semitic they were.

Another student, a junior at City College reported:

> In some of my classes here at City there are some kids who make snide remarks when they see someone wearing a yarmulkah. Sometimes they make these remarks to me too not realizing that I am also an Orthodox Jew even though I don't walk around with a yarmulkah on my head. Also, I have applied to various department stores in New York for jobs and when I tell them I cannot work on Saturday they always say they have no positions open.

Clearly it is necessary to make a distinction between discrimination against Orthodox Jews and against Jews in general, although in some instances one is merely a cover for the other. The following account by a Brooklyn College freshman points to some of the self-image problems Jews have had and continue to have:

> I went to a rough junior high school. Because I was afraid of the kids I didn't wear my star. I lived in an Italian neighborhood and since they were afraid of Italians I let them think I was Italian. The second year I wore a (Jewish) star. I said to myself: "You're an idiot. What are you afraid of?" I felt I had had it up to here. We've been running for the past 5,000 years. One time a kid came up to me, pushed my books out of my hands, and said "Hi ya Jew!" well, we fought. My father was a boxer in the British Army, the Palestinian Brigade, and he taught me some things.

Quite a few students assumed a militant posture when questioned about their Jewishness. In the view of many observers this attitude has become more and more common on many college campuses and is probably due (among other things) to the general rise in recent years of ethnic pride and identification. The following is an example:

> I was at a meeting where a student said: "Us blacks and Puerto Ricans really have to work hard because the Jews have it made. Brooklyn College is a haven for the Jews and the Jews go together with their Jewish teachers." That's not true! I feel the Jews have it made because we work for it.

The final issue raised in these interviews was the possibility of another Holocaust occurring in the United States. Here opinion was almost equally divided. Some believed a repetition of the Holocaust to be unlikely in this country:

> The people today are not as gullible and would not stand for such a thing. Today would be a good time for this with all the world crisis. Yet it won't happen. Besides I can't think of anyone today who is like Hitler. —a 19-year-old sophomore at Brooklyn College.

> No, not in the United States. We're too loyal to our own type of government to give one man that much power. I think Nixon tried to get enough power to take over but was knocked down by the Senate. —a 21-year-old junior at Baruch College.

> People are too intelligent to let that sort of thing happen again and if any people did try it, I'm sure the United Nations or some other peace-keeping force would step in. —a 21-year-old junior at City College.

Before looking at some of the affirmative responses to this question I want to add that this question contained the lowest percentage of "Not sure" responses. This may indicate that many people had already given a good deal of thought to this important issue prior to the interview. Whatever the case, the responses on both sides reflected strongly held views. A second year student at Queens College stated:

> I definitely believe it could happen here especially if there was an economic depression.

Another student at Queens said:

> It could happen again in a case where someone gets power and the masses of people start acting without thinking about what they're doing and just follow the leader. I feel that could really happen.

It is important to keep in mind that these interviews were conducted in the spring and fall of 1973. Since then world opinion has turned increasingly against Israel. Yassir Arafat has been welcomed at the United Nations, and the Soviet-American trade agreement has been cancelled (due, some say, to the Jewish emigration issue). Moreover, men such as former Attorney General William Saxbe and General George Brown have voiced views amounting to unfavorable stereotyping of Jews.

*   *   *·

This study has been an effort to scratch the surface of what is, in this writer's view, a neglected area—namely an understanding of the Holocaust's effects upon a segment of the contemporary Jewish community. Despite the preliminary nature of the results of this research, certain clear and unmistakeable patterns have emerged that merit serious consideration and further study.

Firstly, there can be no doubt that the Holocaust is an area of great interest to Jewish college students. This can be seen from the very high proportion of students who have done some reading on the subject and that such reading was most often done on the students' own initiative. Furthermore, the responses to many questions revealed a great deal of curiosity about the Holocaust. There was almost no feeling that the events of that era are something that ought to be buried and forgotten.

A second important conclusion to emerge from this study was that young Jews today have a serious problem in terms of their self-image, that is at least partly traceable to the Holocaust. Many respondents criticized European Jewry for being cowardly and for not actively resisting its fate. Many students described a distance between "those Jews" and themselves, stating that their reaction would have been a different one. There was a strong sense of shame and resentment at being compelled to bear what they saw as a burden of cowardice on the part of their own people. Noteworthy is the comment of a student at Yale who informed me he was taking a course in Jewish identity because he was "sick and tired of my own picture of the Jew as sniveling coward." However, although most respondents had some general knowledge of the Holocaust, many possessed no detailed knowledge of it. The interviewers probed the respondents and discovered, among other things, a profound lack of understanding both of the difficulty of resistance under the Nazis, and of the existence of such resistance in some concentration camps and European ghettoes.

Moreover, it is clear from the results of this investigation that very little of the available information on the Holocaust is getting through to young Jews. With this in mind I offer the following recommendations:

1.   The Jewish community should pressure boards of education throughout the country to emphasize the teaching of the Holocaust at the elementary, junior high school, and high school levels.

2.   All major Jewish organizations should give top priority to educating their members and the general community about the Holocaust. While several universities and organizations are already somewhat involved in this area, the Holocaust ought to become a primary focus of *all* Jewish organizations, and should be made an integral part of *all* Jewish studies programs throughout the country's colleges.

3.   Qualified speakers should be made available to interested groups in both the Jewish and non-Jewish communities. These ought to include not only well-known scholars and writers, but also the "average" person who lived through this tragic era.

4.   Films such as "Remember Us," "Kapo," and "Night and Fog" ought to be more widely distributed and shown.

5.   Books dealing with resistance during the Holocaust should be made required reading in courses and programs that deal with the Holocaust. Some examples would be *Treblinka* by Jean Francois Steiner, *They Fought Back*, edited by Yuri Suhl, and the *Anthology of Holocaust Literature*, edited by Jacob Glatstein, Israel Knox, and Samuel Margoshes. Jewish resistance should be treated in a sensitive, honest, and balanced manner.

6.   Trips should be organized and made available for people who want to see the arenas of Jewish destruction in Europe. These

trips might be added to the many existing programs that focus on travel to Israel.

7. Social scientists interested in the Jewish community should engage in research that focuses on how the Holocaust has affected the different segments of the Jewish population.

Several of these recommendations are already being carried out to some degree. What I am suggesting is that these efforts be expanded. No doubt some will see this as a useless or even a masochistic attempt to dredge up the past. This is, I believe, a dangerous attitude. The Holocaust is as much a part of Jewish history as the State of Israel. More importantly, there are apparently serious misconceptions concerning the Holocaust that will only be clarified through the extensive dissemination of information and discussion.

In terms of the implications of the Holocaust the results of this study point to a very significant conclusion. Many young Jews today are anxious and uncertain about their position in the United States. A high proportion of respondents expressed the feeling that anti-Semitism in the United States today is widespread. Many claimed to have been victims of anti-Semitism themselves. This anxiety is also manifest in the cynicism on the part of many students concerning the world's reaction to the Holocaust. They were skeptical of the sincerity (and the depth of that sincerity) shown by the Gentile world to the Jewish community in the period following World War II. That many believed a repetition of the Holocaust was possible in America indicates just how tenuously young Jews today see their position in American society.

As a Jew, I find it difficult to treat this subject entirely objectively, in a purely clinical fashion. My decision to focus on this topic was motivated, in large measure by an experience I had several years ago and which I feel provides an appropriate conclusion to this essay.

In the summer of 1972 I had the opportunity to travel through Poland. There I visited Auschwitz. As I got off the steps of the train I noticed that the supporting poles of the station were painted in alternating red and white stripes like pieces of peppermint candy. The litter baskets were shaped in the form of penguins with their mouths open. The atmosphere was a festive one as people waited for the busses to the camp (As a matter of fact, one person on the train, a youth of about 20, informed me that the Auschwitz museum was a beautiful and fascinating place to visit.).

Upon arriving at the camp I was surprised to see that much of it had been preserved. The "Arbeit Macht Frei" sign was still there, as were the barracks (that had once housed the inmates) and several crematoria. Barbed wire surrounded the camp. Inside one of the buildings were exhibits behind glass walls showing human hair, articles of clothing, and various other items that had been in the camp storehouses when Auschwitz was liberated. Yet with the exception of one or two small exhibits (i.e. several prayer shawls suspended on what looked like clothes lines) there was little indication that Jews had been there, much less that they had died there in great numbers. In fact, an English guide book published in Warsaw stated that there were three triangles worn by the various types of camp inmates—green for criminals, yellow for Jews, and red for political prisoners—and that "red triangles were most frequent." An entire hallway about 200 yards long was lined with photographs of former inmates. Not one had a Jewish-sounding name. Possibly the intention of preserving Auschwitz was primarily to portray it as a victory of socialism over fascism. Whatever the case, the extent of the Jewish tragedy at Auschwitz was scarcely visible.

I did not, however, find this nearly as disturbing as the general way in which the Holocaust was treated, an attitude of casualness and callousness that was impossible to miss. A hotel and two restaurants have been built on the premises of the camp. A souvenir stand sold pennants depicting the prison uniform on one side and a drawing of a guard looking out over a barbed wire enclosure on the other. Picture postcards and lapel pins were also available. Little children ran through the halls of a building laughing, shouting, and playing ball where ghastly medical experiments had once been performed. Inside another building were some teenage youths leaning out of a window and listening to popular music on a radio. In general people appeared to regard their visit to the camp as a family outing and a pleasurable experience. As I walked past one of the crematoria I stopped short. A woman of about sixty with a *babushka* on her head had clambered into the crematorium. She smiled broadly as a child of about twelve took her picture. At this point, I left the camp as quickly as possible.

Erica Wanderman

Children and Families of Holocaust Survivors: A Psychological Overview

Thirty years have elapsed since the last surviving victims of the Nazi concentration camps were liberated by advancing Allied armies. Released were the bearers of a unique and tragic experience, men and women whose widely divergent lives were stamped by a common series of overpowering historical events. Those who were interred could not have varied more in terms of socio-cultural, political, and psychological dimensions. Those who survived and were liberated carried with them still the uniqueness of individual lives and experiences, but shared the memories and consequences of events which had rocked the very foundations of these lives. While even these events to which they were exposed varied greatly, they varied within certain limits. At best, their experiences represented a severe strain to existence as we know it; at worst they embodied a nightmarish transformation.

In the years immediately following World War II, a large number of these survivors, finding that most of the families, communities, and institutions they had known had been destroyed, attempted to rebuild their lives in new countries. A wave of emigration followed, with relocation in such countries as Israel, the United States and Canada. Eventually studies began to appear describing the psychological adjustments (and maladjustments) of survivors in their adopted countries. The term "concentration camp survivor syndrome," which was coined by Niederland in 1961, became widely accepted as an accurate description of the difficulties observed in these people.

While the interest in the psychological consequences of the Holocaust has continued to produce more detailed and better documented information on the survivors themselves, relatively little information has been gathered on the families they formed in the post-war world. Many youthful survivors, finding in the post-liberation period that they had lost most of their families and communities, entered hasty, ill-planned marriages in order to alleviate the intense mourning and separation anxiety they were undergoing (Koenig, 1964: Klein, 1971). Establishing new lives and developing families, sometimes for the second time, became of supreme importance in the face of often profound traumatization.

The experiences the survivor parents brought to their new lives also affected the development of their children. Psychotherapists have recently noted the over-representation of children of survivors among adolescent and young adult patients. Both the common difficulties these children bring to treatment and the specific problems they report have raised important questions regarding the effects of concentration camp survival on the second generation.

Trossman (1968) reports on observed stress reactions in adolescent children of survivors treated at the McGill Student Mental Health Clinic. He suggests that in families where at least one parent exhibits even a mild form of the survivor syndrome, adverse effects on the child are to be expected. Such a parent, according to Niederland's description (1961), may be chronically anxious, vigilant, and depressed (beset by physical symptoms) reliving past terrors in repetitive nightmares, racked with guilt over survival while others died and living a socially isolated life. While the initial problems differ, Trossman describes common features in parent-child interaction and the possible consequences of these to the child. The survivor parents appear excessively overprotective and in response, the children either become moderately phobic or rebel. Trossman also speculates that the relating of Holocaust memories may be related to depressive symptomatology in children of survivors.

Survivor parents often expect their children to exhibit an attitude of hostile suspiciousness of the surrounding world similar to their own. When the child is confronted with the irrationality of such an attitude as well as with the suffering which motivated it, conflict ensues. Another parental attitude which Trossman describes is the expectation that children give special meaning to their parents' empty lives: They restitute lost objects, goals, and ideals, and vindicate the suffering the parents have endured. Thus, the child is invested with meanings and expectations which far exceed his own, treated not as an individual but as a symbol of all the parents lack in their own lives and hope to attain through the child. Such expectations, of course, cannot be fulfilled, and many of the students either make repetitive, fruitless attempts or rebel and give up.

Barocas and Barocas (1973), in reporting their observations on adolescent children of survivors in psychotherapy, refer to similar problems and patterns of interaction within the families of survivors. Citing Koenig (1964), they postulate that survivor parents "carry on almost desperate, forced attempts to obtain their own identifications through their children." In using their children to gratify their own conscious or unconscious needs, these parents may undermine autonomous growth. Barocas and Barocas (1973) also hypothesize that since survivors have great difficulty in dealing with their own aggressive impulses, they may unconsciously facilitate the expression of aggression in their children. This may be related to reports of uncontrolled aggressive erupting in adolescent children of survivors. The authors believe that severe depression in children of survivors results from the internalization of anger against parental upbringing. They also speculate that the survivors' repeated encounters with death during the Holocaust are communicated to children in the form of exaggerated overprotectiveness regarding almost any form of activity. Finally, the authors discuss the place of survivor guilt in raising children. They speculate that survivors attempt to alleviate their guilt (i.e. their surviving, while others died) by becoming over-identified with their children. The children of survivors must take on the additional burden of compensating for the parents' sense of worthlessness. As a result these children often show unusually adverse reactions to even inconsequential setbacks and failures. Such failures or frustrations in achievement in part indicate that the child is not fulfilling the task of validating the parents' sense of worth.

Kestenberg (1972) reported on the results of a questionnaire circulated to 320 members of the American Association for Child Psychoanalysis. The questionnaire was directed at gathering information about the analyses of children of survivors. Specific questions of importance were:

    1) Do the children of survivors share common psychological problems?

    2) Are survivor parents' experiences transmitted to the second generation?

    3) If they are, how do they affect children of survivors?

Kestenberg reported that at least twenty analyses of children of survivors have been conducted, with many more therapies and consultations. But because of the personal difficulty they had in listening to concentration camp stories, many analysts themselves showed some resistance to probing the relationship between their patients' difficulties and the survivor parents' experiences.

On the basis of her preliminary data, Kestenberg concluded that there are many variables affecting the survivor parent that are relevant in considering possible effects on raising children. It is necessary, for example, to assess the extent of psychological damage to the patient with regard to his age, type and duration of persecution, traumatization, and pre- and post-Holocaust experiences. It is therefore of primary importance to understand exactly what is meant by such terms as "survivor's child" and "survivor parents." Kestenberg suggests that the term "survivor's child" applies to an individual, not necessarily a child, who was born after the Holocaust, and, while not himself subject to persecution, but is the child of at least one parent who was subject to persecution.

Her definition of "survivor parent" is a much more complex one. Included are people who survived the Nazi Holocaust in either concentration camps, ghettoes or through difficult hiding, and who, as a result, share some psychological characteristics relevant to raising children. All survivor parents have experienced extreme rejection and denigration by their environment, often resulting in a corresponding feeling of self-hatred. This may have been especially detrimental to adolescents and may affect their roles as parents of adolescents. If this self-hatred is not reversed by a more positive self-image after the war, survivor parents run the risk of presenting themselves to their children as "worthless" (and expecting their children to redeem their denigrated identity through special deeds). The exposure to sadistic realities and incomplete mourning for important lost objects, institutions, and a past self may also interfere with certain integrative functions necessary for successful child rearing.

A pilot study was conducted by Sigal and Rakoff (1971) in order to empirically validate some of the clinically observed effects of concentration camp survival on the second generation. All of the survivors they studied shared at least one of the following: 1) symptoms of severe depression with some attempted suicides; 2) school problems; 3) excessive quarreling among siblings. In their study the authors compared thirty-two families of survivors to twenty-four families of controls (i.e. parents not under Nazi persecution during the Holocaust). All were families who had applied for psychological help for their child. All parents were Jewish immigrants from Central Europe. The survivor group included families in which one or both parents were survivors of a Nazi concentration camp, and/or had lost their own parents in a camp. The control group parents fulfilled neither of these two criteria. All children were born after the persecution.

Results indicated that survivor families: 1) exhibited significantly more difficulty in controlling their children; 2) evidenced a significantly greater tendency to overvalue their child (the patient); and 3) complained significantly more about fights between siblings. However, survivor families did not exhibit more dysphoria (depression) in the home, and their children did not have a higher incidence of school problems. Sigal and Rakoff speculate that when difficulties arise in survivor families, they may follow an identifiable pattern. The survivors' difficulty with controlling children is related to a preoccupation with past terrors, and a consequent depletion and lack of flexibility and readaptation necessary for child-rearing. The survivor parents respond to their child's need for attention by pleading that he stop being a claim on them. The child, in turn, finding his needs inappropriately met, responds with disruptive behavior, depression, and anxiety. Since much guilt is invoked in opposing a parent who has already suffered so much, the anger that children feel is more easily displaced in sibling fighting. The parents, in their turn, perceive their children as difficult to control and excessively quarrelsome.

Based on the above findings, Sigal, Silver, Rakoff, and Ellin (1973) undertook a more extensive study. The authors hypothesized that children of survivors would differ from controls in the areas of 1) impulse control (particularly the control of aggression); and 2) in a sense of anomie and alienation. The study revealed that survivor parents rated their adolescent children significantly higher in conduct problems, personality problems, inadequacy-maturity, excessive dependence, limit-testing, and poor coping behavior. Thus, survivor-parents perceive their adolescent children as being significantly more disturbed than control parents perceive their children. In discussing their findings, the authors speculate that some of the difficulties of children of survivors become especially marked in adolescence. Many of the personality or developmental problems were understood by the authors to be a result of parental preoccupation. Already taxed resources make it impossible for these parents to provide adequate and appropriate feedback to their children. The children, in turn, become anxious and disruptive, and have special difficulties in identification. The consequence of identifying with a depressed, uprooted parents may be the child's own depression and alienation. The consequence of not identifying with a survivor parent to whom this is crucial is often guilt, which may also contribute to depression and alienation.

Rustin (1973) reports on a study of guilt, hostility and Jewish identification among sixty 17 to 22 year-old children of concentration camp survivors. The author hypothesizes that children of survivors, as a result of their parents' experiences, will suffer from more guilt than other children. Further, in identifying with their parents, they will, as do their parents, have greater difficulty in expressing aggression and hostility. Also in the course of identifying with their parents, these adolescents will be more invested in Jewish identification. Results indicated that adolescent children of survivors score higher on guilt, although not significantly so. They did not indicate that they had greater difficulty in expressing hostility. Jewish identification was higher for children of survivors than for controls.

Klein (1971), in Israel, undertook a study of survivor families living in a kibbutz setting. He found that even before their birth, the children of survivor parents were viewed as a source of security and gratification, an undoing of destruction, and a restoration of lost family. Many survivor mothers experienced fantasies of damage about themselves and their child during pregnancy. Klein speculated that in cases where this fear was overwhelming, it was acted out in amenorrhea, miscarriage, and sterility. This appears to support Krystal's (1971) report of the puzzlingly high abortion rate among women survivors. Some fears of damage continued to rise into the early mother-child relationship. In the infancy of the child particularly, both parents seemed to live in fear of something happening to the child. Unconscious as well as conscious exaggerated fears of separation are apparent in both parents and children. These become more conscious in danger situations such as war or children's illnesses, when parents engage in such compulsive behavior as frequent night-time checking of the child. The parents have repetitive nightmares of concentration camp experiences in which the children are also present and in danger of being separated from them. The children clearly share in their parents' fear of separation. They spend significantly more time with their families than the average kibbutz child. Overt expression of anger toward parents is avoided. When confronted with open aggression or danger, these children tend to react passively by escaping, hiding, holding on to other children, or seeking adult help. In terms of their parents' experiences, children of survivors tend to emphasize the heroic aspects of the parents' past, negating or denying the suffering. A protectiveness of the parents for their special experiences is also noted.

It appears, then, that as people and as parents, concentration camp survivors suffer from numerous difficulties, some of which are more likely to affect their children than others. The following sketch emerges of a survivor mother who may suffer from symptoms of the survivor syndrome. Her ability to respond appropriately to her growing child, to set limits, tease out curiosity and accept robust activity is severely impaired by her own difficulties. In many ways she is not unlike a mother preoccupied for different reasons (Sigal, 1974; Rakoff, Sigal, and Epstein, 1967). Her special experience in a concentration camp, however, may contribute (even before pregnancy) to her viewing the birth of a child as a reversal of her own encounter with death and destruction. The hope of restitution of lost objects, strivings and ideals is revived by the birth of a child at the same time that the fear of damage and perpetuation of stigma are revived by the reality of pregnancy (Klein, 1973). While the infant is a drain on the mother who is still mourning for herself and others, it also briefly provides a symbiotic restitution. But already fears of separation and loss include the infant and impose onto its life events which have meaning only in the mothers' (Lipkowitz, 1973). The child is overvalued, invested with meanings that are different from his own resources and abilities. The enactment by the child of the parents' wishes is viewed as a crucial ingredient to the parents' psychological survival. To this end, the child is excessively nagged and excessively humored, but always with the view that he must be hammered into an identity useful to the parents. The recounting of terrifying memories by the parents sometimes enters into the child's life. Even without this direct aspect, the parents' self-presentation of suffering makes aggression against them by the child difficult and guilt-inducing. The outside world is often viewed and presented by the parent as imminently dangerous and hostile, and pressure is strong on the child to accept this view in the service of survival.

A sketch of the survivor's child emerges which is commensurate with some of the above. This child, in response to maternal preoccupation, sometimes becomes anxious and disorganized in some of his capacities, exhibits difficulty in self-control, gives in to irrational impulses, is depressed, and lacks an appropriate involvement in the world. Special difficulty with separation between mother and child is often mirrored in the child's acute anxiety about separation, and excessive dependency on his parents. The child may also have extreme fears of the outside world, which is presented as dangerous and hostile. The burden of compensating for parental losses and empty lives creates a multitude of difficulties, particularly during adolescence. A prolonged and difficult crisis may result, in which more aspects of the adolescent's functioning are affected than under normal circumstances. For example, an identification with a parent's depressive outlook, sense of damage, and vigilant fearfulness may be related to similar conscious and unconscious feelings on the part of the child. These may be expressed in a sense of emptiness and alienation from the surrounding culture and activities. A struggle not to accept such an identification may lead to feelings of guilt about betraying a parent to whom this is all-important. The child's sensitivity to his parents' suffering may lead to a guilt-ridden protectiveness of them. Any acting out of aggression toward the parent becomes problematical, as does the acknowledgment of aggression and conflict in general. If the child identifies with the parents as victims, aggression is a danger which is either denied, or met passively. On the other hand, the parent may be viewed as a super-human hero, thereby causing the child's self-image to include feelings of elitism or chosen descendancy.

The review of current literature in the area of second generation effects of concentration camp survival points to the fact that investigation in this area is just beginning. Most of the studies thus far consist of clinical observations of survivor families and children. The small number of empirically based studies that exist suffer from problems in sampling, definition of terms, and methodology. With a generation of children of Holocaust survivors now coming of age and presenting us with their special problems, sensibilities and strengths, further study of the long-term psychological effects of the Holocaust is crucial. Research directed at understanding the post-war adjustment of survivors and their families is the responsibility of the scientific and academic communities to this and other traumatized populations.

Bibliography

1. Barocas, H. and Barocas, C., "Manifestations of Concentration Camp Effects on the Second Generation," *American Journal of Psychiatry*, Vol. 130, No. 7 (1973), pp. 821-21

2. Bettelheim, B., "Individual and Mass Behavior in Extreme Situations," *Journal of Abnormal Social Psychology*, Vol. 38 (1943), pp. 417-52

3. Frankl, V., *The Doctor and the Soul: An Introduction to Logotherapy*, New York, Alfred A. Knopf, 1955

4. Kestenberg, J., "Psychoanalytic Contributions to the Problem of Children of Survivors from Nazi Persecution," *The Israel Annals of Psychiatry and Related Disciplines*, Vol. 10, No. 4 (1972), pp. 311-325

5. Klein, H., "Families of Survivors in the Kibbutz: Psychological Studies" in H. Krystal and W. Niederland, eds., *Psychic Traumatization* (Vol. 8 of *International Psychiatry Clinics*), Boston, Little, Brown, and Co., 1971, pp. 67-92

6. _____, "Children of the Holocaust: Mourning and Bereavement" in "Children of the Holocaust," *International Yearbook of Child Psychiatry* (J. Anthony, ed.), Vol. 12 (1974), pp. 393-409

7. Koenig, W., "Chronic or Persisting Identity Diffusion," *American Journal of Psychiatry*, Vol. 120 (1964), pp. 1081-1084

8. Krystal, H., "Trauma: Considerations of its Intensity and Chronicity" in H. Krystal and W. Niederland, eds., *Psychic Traumatization* (Vol. 8 of *International Psychiatry Clinics*) Boston, Little, Brown and Co., 1971, pp. 11-28

9. Lipkowitz, M., "The Child of Survivors: A Report of an Unsuccessful Therapy," *The Israel Annals of Psychiatry and Related Disciplines*, Vol. 2, No. 2 (1973), pp. 141-55

10. Niederland, W., "The Problem of the Survivor," *Journal of Hillside Hospital*, No. 10 (1961), pp. 222-247

11. Rakoff, V., Sigel, J. and Epstein, N., "Children and Families of Concentration Camp Survivors," *Canada's Mental Health*, Vol. 14 (1967), pp. 24-26

12. Rustin, S., "Guilt, Hostility and Jewish Identification Amongst Adolescent Children of Concentration Camp Survivors," Unpublished Doctoral Dissertation, New York University, 1971

13. Sigel, J., "Second-Generation Effects of Massive Psychic Trauma," in H. Krystal and W. Niederland, eds., *Psychic Traumatization* (Vol. 8 of *International Psychiatry Clinics*), Boston, Little, Brown, and Co., pp. 55-65

14. Sigel, J. and Rakoff, V., "Concentration Camp Survival: A Pilot Study of Effects on the Second Generation," *Canada's Mental Health*, Vol. 14 (1967), pp. 24-26

15. Sigel, J., Silver, D., Rakoff, V., and Ellin, B., "Some Second-Generation Effects of Survival of the Nazi Persecution," *American Journal of Orthopsychiatry*, Vol. 43, no. 3 (1973), pp. 320-327

16. Trossman, B., "Adolescent Children of Concentration Camp Survivors," *Canada Psychiatric Association Journal*, Vol. 13 (1968), pp. 121-23

"Untitled," William Aron, Photographer

Hans Herda

CONSIDER MY LIFE:
An Essay on Becoming Jewish

Israel the country is surrounded as never before by hostile currents. The steady physical hatred of her Arab neighbors has been augmented by a swelling ideological denunciatory chorus from third-world countries, with generous assistance from the Soviet Union and from China. Now the economic politics of King Oil and the lure of Arab investment have prodded so-called free nations of western Europe to turn their backs on Israel as well. The State of Israel rose from the ashes of one holocaust, and I believe it will not die except as the victim of another.

The European Holocaust caused many events, great and minor, far beyond the imagination of its architects. Consider my life: I was born a Protestant Lutheran in Berlin, in 1938. I grew up in Berlin during and after the war, entirely without knowledge of the Jews and all those foul murders. My historical studies in the Volksschule in Berlin-Neukoelln included Greece and Rome as well as mediaeval Germany, but Bismarck and the Hohenzollerns, the World Wars and Hitler and his gang did not exist in my textbooks. I had competent teachers who (as I now understand) avoided those topics. I lived with my divorced mother and her mother — and they never touched on the fate of the Jews. My mother was no friend of the Nazi regime, hence our bookshelves gave no clues to recent history.

Even then I was aware of dark secrets. I was a first-grader in 1944. Along with reading and writing we learned to fold our hands and say a prayer for the Reichsfuehrer. I still recall one couplet: ... gib zu seinem schweren Werke / unserm Fuehrer Kraft und Staerke ... (give our Fuehrer power and strength for his heavy labor). Who was this man whose pictures, swastikas and brownshirts had been everywhere? I had rocked undetonated bombs in the streets, had seen machine guns and bazookas thrown away like so much garbage at the end. I had watched the looting and the delirious fear before the Russian troops moved in. But then they played with me and one of them dandled me on his knee. It was my first awareness of the big Nazi lie.

In 1951 my mother and I emigrated to Detroit. Again, I went to school for years without learning the awful truth. I commuted by bus to the inner-city Cass Technical High School and there met a number of Jews, some of whom became my lasting friends. But these were social contacts. As a freshman at Wayne State University I discovered the Kasle Judaica Collection, and the recent Jewish past hit me full-force. In my undergraduate years I spent many afternoons with the Kasle books. I read widely and deeply in history, philosophy and theology, began to study Yiddish and Hebrew, joined the campus B'nai B'rith Hillel group — in other words, I prepared for becoming a "ger tzedek," a convert to Judaism.

A few years later, a "bet din" (Jewish court) affirmed my Jewishness. I married Phyllis. My family lives Jewishly; my children are only faintly puzzled that I was not born Jewish and that Oma (grandma) is a Christian. We are active members of Temple Emunah in Lexington, Massachusetts, we enjoy Shabbat at Havurat Shalom in Somerville, and we participate in communal retreats with the other East Coast havurot. It is a minor history, but what Nazi functionary could have dreamed of it? And there are a few thousand like me sprinkled across the world, a new diaspora, another mantle for the Torah that is the house of Israel. Some of them even "daven" in Berlin.

I am a child of the Holocaust. I was spared, but my people died. When the time for mourners' kaddish comes I do not rise, but I say the kaddish quietly and think of them. Had there been no Holocaust, would I be Jewish now? It is an empty question. I am a Jew of the Holocaust and it will be mine to confront while I live and think. My bond with the Holocaust enables and shapes this essay.

Factual, personal confrontation with the Holocaust is relatively easy. The Nazis made a table of conquered Europe and ate up Jewry as the chief meal. It is not so simple in the poetic realm. Nelly Sachs, Andre Schwarz-Bart and Elie Wiesel come to mind as notable interpreters of the horror. Others are still to be heard. After all, Barbara Tuchman now writes with insight about World War I, while

Solzhenitsyn and Kuznetsov unearth the Soviet past. I now understand why the Holocaust has had little influence on the prayer book, although many congregations incorporate it in special readings for Rosh ha-Shanah and Yom Kippur. The wound is still healing, the historical perspective foreshortened. How can the mind grasp the meaning of six million martyrs? There is no neat formula. Each Jewish group, each generation, will try to digest the Holocaust in its own way.

I have before me the German *Pessach-Buch* (Passover-Book), dedicated "to the first freedom- and spring-festival of the remainder of Israel in Europe" in 1946.* It is a remarkable collection containing source materials, accounts of Passover in ancient times, cuts from manuscripts and printed haggadot, Passover stories by Agnon, Bialik, Buber, Heine, Mendele Mocher Sforim, Peretz and others, as well as the moving dialogue of a survivor with his conscience. Four Passover songs are printed at the end: chad gadya, adir hu, am yisrael chai — and hatikva. Its message is clear: across the centuries Passover is the holiday that celebrates the freedom of the Jews and the end of the Holocaust.

Visual interpretation of the Holocaust is essential. I have seen many photographs of the concentration camps, but they all numb my spirit and fade away, only to haunt me in dreams. My humanity is made firmer when I look at the art work of the camp inmates. Gerald Green's *The Artists of Terezin* (New York, Hawthorn Books, Inc., 1969) has very accomplished art and a good literary commentary. But the art of amateurs has the greater power to command attention in this setting. *The Book of Alfred Kantor* (New York, McGraw-Hill Book Co., 1971) shows the bare bones of Terezin, Auschwitz, and Schwarzheide from within. And . . . *I never saw another butterfly . . .* (McGraw-Hill Book Co., N.Y., 2nd ed., 1971) presents children's drawings and poems from Terezin. Of the 15,000 children under age 15 who passed through, only about 100 survived. Yet their works, affirming the value of life and the worldwide oneness of the human condition, are antidotes to hatred and despair.

The nature of present Jewish and Gentile attitudes to the

---

*Israel Blumenfeld, ed. *Pessach-Buch* (Marburg, Germany, *Juedische Rundschau* [newspaper], 1946) Blumenfeld was a historian of the Warsaw ghetto.

destruction of European Jewry is complex and diffuse. What have we learned from the horrible history of Nazism? In 1960, a well-meaning friend of my mother, whom I visited in Bonn, urged me not to "ally myself with the Jews." He did not like the Jews, and for him it was impossible to think that I might become one. To my mother I have long been a Jew. But she is fearful for my life; that I have joined a people that has been the object of persecution for centuries. She feels that I, as a Jew, will always be in danger.

Josef Goebbels once said, "There are those ideas which the Reich furthers, those which it rejects, and those which it roots out." Among the first to go was what Albert Schweitzer called reverence for life. Our government lost it early on the way to My Lai; it is often lost, in east and west, and in the third and fourth worlds. But decency can be recovered, and reverence for life along with it. If we work hard to advance humane caring our nation may never sink to the level of Nazi Germany.

I sense implications for me and for my family here. I cannot control my government much, though I try to influence it. But I can be open, loving and caring — and not just to Jews. I must be gentle with my children so that they may learn to be loving. They know I have prejudices, but these do not wipe out my concern. And, above all, I care deeply for Israel.

What is the official German government response to the Holocaust? The West German and Israeli governments have been politically and economically quite friendly since Dr. Adenauer's accession to the chancellorship in 1949. The restitution treaty of 1953 and large-scale subsequent aid to Israel, as well as the Federal Republic's action as a clandestine arms conduit between the U.S. and Israel from 1959 to 1964 attest to this reality. The German Democratic Republic echoes the Soviet bloc accusation of Israel as an outpost of capitalist neocolonialism, a puppet of the United States. But when I traveled in Germany in 1960, I found that the East German customs officers routinely confiscated anti-Semitic books while Federal Republic customs waived them through.

Even murkier is the picture seen by the general traveler. Ruth and Peter Gay write in "Musings in Munich" (*The American Scholar*, Winter 1974-75, pp. 41-51) about the pleasures and the urbanity of Munich life, and quote Jews in Munich as saying that "Germany is the least anti-Semitic country in the world." My wife and I traveled in Europe in 1972 and we found evident nostalgia for Hitler and his regime among older people in Munich. It was exceeded (in our experience) only in Salzburg. Perhaps one finds what one seeks, by a process of semi-conscious pre-selection of conversations and experiences. I know that some of the murderers walk the streets; alas, they are aging. Some of their children have gone to work in kibbutzim, a few have gone my way, others adhere to the hatreds of their parents. Most of them probably steer an oblivious middle course. In Germany there is a real generation gap of silence, despite more recent student enlightenment about the Nazi era and genuine academic interest in Jewish institutions.

There have always been friends as well as enemies of the Jews in Germany and Austria. I cannot assess their relative strength. Admiration for militant Israel has been widespread, though it seems to have become more cautious in the last year. In any case, it is not confined to friends of the Jews. The anti-Semites are not saying or doing much. Anti-Semitism is outlawed and recent history weighs heavily. Besides, the Jewish population is a good deal smaller than before the war and the old lies just can't be made to stick in public. Ironically, Germany the Judenrein has become safe for the Jews. But who among us will settle there?

In the center of Lexington I sometimes see the painted school bus of the White Peoples' Party/American Nazi Party passing by. The party is neither a joke nor a mass movement. To me, that bus and its meaning right now is not nearly as important as masses of Jews living Jewish lives is important. Anti-Semitism must be fought, but Jewishness must also be preserved and enriched. We must work to strengthen Israel the country as well as Jewish existence in the United States and around the world. And we must start with ourselves.

"American Sorrow," William Aron, Photographer

Liliane Richman

FROM THE FAMILY ALBUM

I stare at the photographs displayed all over my bedroom. There, Mary Pickford-like, my mother holds a bouquet of white lilies. I marvel at her elegance, at the coy confident smile, whose reality I never witnessed, murdered, raped in a land of nightmares. She did not tell her story too often.

"I sold all my jewelry and bought salamis and cookies and canned asparagus, anything that could be had on the black market. He was a prisoner of war and I had been advised that I might be able to see him before his company was sent out to some German prison camp. I left your brother with the neighbors. I was eight months pregnant and very big. I traveled on the train nine hours. I got there. It was cold, grey I remember. I went to the barbed wire gate, asked if the prisoners could be visited. The French guard said, 'My poor woman they left last night.' I stood there awhile crying and made my way back to Paris."

She spoke in a monotone as if her narrative was not an unusual story, a story only the prelude to more sinister events, but already muted, softened by time. I always listened attentively to the grown-ups whenever they talked about their past.

* * *

My mother, this blonde beautiful woman, who miraculously survived an even bleaker adulthood than those deprived childhoods, is smiling again on the next photograph. She is posing with her son in a professional photographer's studio, smiling in nineteen forty in the occupied city where black-booted conquerors test their theory of unequal races. Because of that incomprehensible smile, I grew up forgiving her, her tyrannical petty temper unintentionally bent on revenging herself for particular abuses she suffered as a Jewish woman. Soon after sitting with my older brother in the photographer's studio one November morning, she walked to Hotel Dieu hospital to give birth. The dry monotonous sound of bombs tack, tack, tack accompanied her loneliness. I have grown to thirty with children of my own and have never spoken to her about those days when she was my age, she then, I now, when we are sisters.

And am I to exploit her now as a subject to train my pen on? Writers compose stories from the realities provided by their era. I cannot depict the comfortable tedium of daily life; it is not quite the right sequence to speak of the laughter of children, the warmth of voices, the tenderness of shared recurrences in the small of the morning, the shuffling gait of old people in the green of Spring. My growing up was filled with musings about peacetime, its meaning and its relationship to war. I reflected about peace, this time of triumph which paradoxically produces people serving time routinely, their energies chained to an epoch disillusioned by ideas and systems born in previous centuries yet persisting and emerging from the turmoils of wholesale death. I wondered why with hunger satisfied and children growing up with the assurance of inheriting a safe future so many human beings remained disenchanted and unhappy. Like a serpent eating its own tail I thought that wars were bred on such propitious cultures with death and despair consuming dull ennui, with the sad people of yesterday galvanized by action and turned into heroes. I was haunted with the idea that perhaps those heroes of all resistances who survive look back on apocalyptic time with longing as for a lost paradise in the wistful manner of the mechanic thirsting for his brutal childhood. They were alive then, unhampered by the dry rot of routine, when each day had to be wrenched out of death and created boldly. Such people say, "an eternity of idyllic poetry is a bore, a bourgeois dream." They lust for action, action at all costs with the gun and the pen, the pamphlet, the muscles and the flesh, with power over a friend, at anyone's expense.

My memories, rather the absence of my memories of those first critical childhood years, have been filled in with the impoverished details provided by a few persons that I should have learned to know better. There will be no Proustian cup of tea for me. My taste buds, unable to recall, have absorbed no essence, no pattern on which I might try to root my life, to lift it out of its unknown tempos. I play at assembling a puzzle ignorant yet of its parts and contents.

*　　*　　*

I could not have learned from the photographs on my night table that French policemen had come to arrest her. I shuddered in disbelief when years later I asked for details. I could not accept the idea of my own countrymen collaborating with the racial policies of their own enemy — history had too insistently taught me that France was the land of liberty, equality and fraternity for all. Since then I have witnessed Chileans murdering other Chileans and Russians shut away, assaulted in their last retreat, the inner core of their brain, dehumanised by Russian psychiatrists.

They questioned her first, "Where are your children? You have a boy of eight and a baby girl. We won't harm them. You'll see, you will all be reunited and relocated. Don't be afraid." Click! Blonde, slender, no photograph today to witness her eternal smile stretching from one end to the other of the black-booted grid in front of her. They take her away to the central stadium, this Vel d'hiv where other Jews are waiting with shapeless bundles, the last shreds of their former individuality. She had been here once with Stephane to watch a dizzying game of soccer. The speed, the loud colors of the rival teams echo in today's gloom. Presently another game is played in the stadium, death in the arena, the flamenco, the corrida, today's performance orchestrated by black boots.

*　　*　　*

No pictures of these next four years, only my conjectures and my embarrassed questions. "I need this information. I'm writing a story." She wrote back.

"I dedicate this to you my daughter. It is difficult for me to write, I am not smart enough, I couldn't finish school you see, my parents took me out so I could work at home. I don't know how to express myself. It is a terrible thing for me to go through; telling it.

I was arrested by the French police, taken to Drancy, and then to Bergen Belsen. Your father was already a prisoner. You knew him when you were five, after the war. When you were born I was alone with your older brother. You were so small and so pretty. I forgot many things. Then to save your life and your brother's I had to send you away not knowing if I would ever see you again. I was nobody, alone in this big city at war. In the concentration camp I called for death many times. Though constantly around it did not come for me, I don't know why, with the winter, the lack of clothing and food, the forced labor and the desolation. I was in a coma for six days when we were liberated. I survived. Many things happened before we were reunited. What's the good of talking about it? I am nearly sixty and I worry about my heart and this pacemaker. They are going to operate on me again. Life is a bitch, I'd hate to relive mine . . . Kiss David and the children.''

Once more she did not tell me anything I hadn't known. She had picked up her life where it had been snatched from her, concealing the scars as best she could, though they had made no truce with her. After the four year lapse, she frequented anew the photographer's studio. On the next picture in the photo album the Pickfordian grace has vanished. Back from an ordeal from which nothing could be gained, no initiation rite (you know what they say about the suffering, the redemption and the grace, the arrow and the creative wound). She was a stout woman smiling the solidified grin of established roles and mores. Her children next to her are clean, serious. She taught them what she knew — that life is no sweet cornucopia — but gave them no record of her living nightmares, while daily reality inexorably spans routine, sustaining even such atrophied life.

*　　　*　　　*

The photo essay assembled on my night table is not complete without mention of my father. All my friends fell in love with him. She warned me once with words that remained a red shame long after I had heard them. "All men are alike, beasts forcing themselves on us, your father too." He came to meet me after the war, made his way to the southwest by train. He looked foreign as he stood in the railway station with his dark unassimilated gypsy look. A native examined him closely, "What do you want here?"

"I come back from the war to get my children. Whereabout is Sabres?" "You can only get there by bus and the last one left. How about a drink?" They talked about the war. The dark man recounted how he had been a prisoner of war in Germany, how the men in his outfit more than once ate their own feces. He spoke about his wife;

he did not yet know whether she survived the concentration camp. He expressed his tormented anguish at the thought of soon meeting his two children, one of whom he had never seen. The southerner simply drove him to his destination without another word.

*   *   *

"You were poor when you were young," murmurs my own daughter, "tell me about the war?" I pull out my album of photographs. We both look at the child I was in the midst of the turmoil; I am astonished to be a grown-up, wondering as I did about the solidity of reality. I have long ago come to the last edge-colored page of the pudgy diary which I started as a child. I am not yet a novelist, nor a poet, nor a singer, nor an actress but still want to be. I am the intellectual of the family, the only one to attend a university, a phenomenon I owe to my settling in the United States. I read my child the gory adventures of Odysseus of Ithaca; we both watch Asians on their long trails of sorrow and death. My little girl screams, "Why?" and "It isn't fair" and, "Do women kill and murder too, or is it just men?" I have no qualms today when the beds stay unmade and the floors unswept. I have both successfully remembered and forgotten the legacy my mother bequeathed me. I go visit my parents across that enormous ocean whenever I can with a great eruption in my heart. We argue about sex and contraception. My mother feels that sex should not be free, that one should pay for the pleasures of the flesh.

In her last letter she has written, "All my children are happy, I shall die with a feeling of accomplishment." Of course it isn't true; if it were I would not understand her lack of bitterness, but she is older and needs the justification. As I gaze at the photograph on the night table by my bedside she smiles, still beautiful, a mother, a wife, a victim of her times, and I love her, I love her.

"Returning," William Aron, Photographer

Hannah Levinsky Koevary

A SEARCH FOR HOME
The Road to Israel

For my grandparents, in loving memory

The Yahrzeit candles which were kindled in my home several times a year told me the story I already knew. The yellow reflection flickered on the ceiling, dancing and swaying, first growing larger then smaller. The flames seemed to burn forever, always there, reminding me that they replaced the graves of my grandparents which never existed. On Tisha B'Av, my parents would light candles for the others in their family who died without a time or a place. I remember Yom Kippur: the kitchen table was covered with those candles. There must have been at least 15 or 20 of them, standing on a thin sheet of metal, so as not to burn a hole in the white tablecloth. They never did. The only hole that they burned was in me.

I always knew what the candles represented. I never asked my parents. It seemed as if the answers were always there. As each year passed, I learned that the flames stood for names. Then later, I was told the details, and then sometimes the reasons.

I learned that there was a place called concentration camp, a term which I never heard outside my home until I was much older. I knew that these were places where Jews were taken and from which they rarely returned. Whatever I knew, my parents told me. There were stories filled with sadness, pain and nostalgia. My mother would evoke the piety of her father, the brilliance of her older brother, the wisdom of her mother. I often heard her say how the war obliterated all that and how things would never be the same. One day while my mother was walking me to Hebrew school in the middle of winter, I asked her why Hitler killed my grandparents. My mother could not answer the question. She began to cry and I cried with her. It was the first and last time I asked that question. I was seven years old.

There were other reminders of what my parents went through. If words were not spoken then it was gestures which communicated the Event. I remember one Friday while my mother was preparing for the Sabbath. She stood above the open flame of the stove burning off the remainder of the feathers from a chicken. I saw the fire singe her hand. She did not move, nor wince. "Mommy, doesn't that hurt you?" I asked. She looked at me for a long time. "This is nothing," she said and continued her work. "I've been through worse." I knew what she meant and didn't need an explanation, nor did I ever ask again.

Perhaps it was because I heard so much about my grandparents and aunts and uncles that I felt their absence so much. My parents' friends and the small remnant of cousins who survived the war became my substitute for the others. These were the people whom we would meet on Sundays and other occasions. We all passed through the good and bad times together: living in rough neighborhoods, moving to better ones; getting sick, getting well; celebrating birthdays and Bar Mitzvahs; enjoying summers, overcoming winters.

I was always happy in their presence. Whenever we got together we would eat and drink and play and laugh. I always had a good time with them. The joys and successes of the children occupied most of their lives and we all felt it. There was a kind of closeness between child and parent which I have rarely seen elsewhere. The girls shared a special intimacy with their mothers and the boys were never embarrassed to kiss their fathers in public. I always heard them speak about the past, their home, and hometown. If they discussed the tales of horror it was never in front of us.

It was these people — my parents, their friends and children — who represented my Jewish world. It was safe, warm, secure. But between the Sundays, summers in the country and special occasions, my childhood was spent among Gentiles who constantly reminded me that their world was closed to Jews. It was an Italian/Irish/German neighborhood in Brooklyn, surrounded by Churches and adorned with crucifixes. Seasons were marked by Christmas, Easter, Halloween, Saints' days and meatless Fridays. The smell of evergreen and pine filled the air from November to January, while the scent of palm branches and tulips dominated March and April, only giving way to black and orange candy with frightening costumes and masks in late October. The songs I learned in school were mixtures of patriotic American hymns and Christian songs, always introduced with a passage from the New Testament. I was the only Jew in my public school. Three years later another Jew entered: my sister.

I played with my Catholic friends but learned very quickly that what separated me from them was something that allegedly happened two thousand years ago.

"You killed Christ," they would tell me over and over again. For my crime, prohibitions were made and enforced. When we would play with cardboard boxes to erect playhouses, I could not enter theirs. "Jews are not allowed in," my friends would tell me, laughing. So unprovoked were these remarks that they frightened me. My Catholic friends, after returning from Saturday confessions, would confide in me that their priest forbade them to play with me, talk to me, even look my way. They continued to play with me, but to placate their consciences and remove their sins they reminded me who I was and the grandeur of my crime.

I had a friend whose mother actually washed out her daughter's mouth with soap in my presence because she once said "hell." But days later when she called me dirty Jew, kike, Jew bastard, her mother did nothing. In fact, she joined her daughter in the shouts.

I did not need warnings from my parents against Gentile wrath to tell me what I already knew. It made sense to me. Jews were killed for being Jews less than ten years before; why should it change now? The same irrational hatred that murdered my grandparents separated me from my environment. People still hated Jews and were making them suffer for it. My parents' experiences during the War were made more real to me. And my experiences were even more real to them.

My Christian neighbors did not stop at words. Often words led to other things. One day during a heavy snowstorm the mother of my Catholic friend threw a chunk of ice at me and called me Jew-bastard. My face was red and burning, swelled from the hard frozen ice, as both mother and daughter continued their action, alternating between the ice and the words. Moments later my Catholic friend was looking down at her feet, staring at her tooth that rested in the snow and at the bright drops of blood that were a reminder to her not to call me Jew-bastard again.

So ended a bitter chapter, a chapter where my sister had become my only real friend.

A year later we moved . . . this time to an all-Jewish

neighborhood. At last I thought I would receive what I wanted: a Jewish environment, where to be a Jew was not a stigma. My expectations were soon shattered. I learned that the Jewishness of my new acquaintances barely bound them to each other, let alone me to them. I was different and I knew why. My parents were different and I knew how. The others did not even come close to understanding what I felt. For the first time I confronted Jews whose experiences didn't even approximate my own, either in reality or in imagination. To be a stranger among Jews was worse than to be hated by Gentiles. Here I had met Jews whose inner life was a desert and who were exiled from their past — and didn't even know it.

When I tried to gain entry into their world they only reminded me how far I was from them, and when I tried to bring them into mine, they only reminded me how far they were from me.

I was in eighth grade. It was several months after I moved into the new neighborhood. I took the day off from school to become an American citizen. The day I returned to school my teacher asked me to stand up in class. "We'd like to welcome you as a citizen of the United States of America," he said. Explaining that I was born in Germany and had immigrated as a young child, he then instructed the class on the meaning of citizenship. The eyes of my classmates, partly laughing, mostly derisive, were on me. My face was red and hot. I felt humiliated as I sat down. Later my Jewish classmates called me Nazi and Hitler in mocking tones and greeted me with 'Sieg Heil.' It was the names they would use in jest. Among the Jews I was a Nazi, and among the Gentiles I was Jew. How could I tell them who Hitler was or what Hitler did? In class we never discussed that there ever was a war in which Jews were slaughtered. It was a hidden event which remained mine alone for many years.

I was either 14 or 15 when I first heard the word "refugee" being used to describe my parents and others like them. The Jewish people on the block would use it in passing, not giving weight or thought to the word. In my mind, refugees were people who were haggard and poor. My parents and their friends jokingly would call themselves 'greener.' But the others called us refugees and soon even those who didn't call us that thought it.

One day at a friend's house the conversation turned to my parents and the war.

"You know those refugees really expect everything on a golden platter," my friend's mother said to me. "They push and demand. They all have money and want more of it."

Could I believe my ears? Was this a Jewish woman speaking? I couldn't find words to respond to her accusations.

"But of course *your* parents are different," she reassured me. "They're not like the other refugees." I could no longer contain my anger.

"How dare you speak that way?" My throat was already hoarse and my eyes swelling with tears. "Do you know how they suffered? What if you lost your entire family — your relatives, friends, and neighbors in a death camp? How dare you judge them?"

She looked at me mockingly. "Don't tell me about suffering. We went through the Depression. Don't think that we didn't suffer in America." She went on to tell me about the vegetarian meals, the jobless days, the silk stocking-less ladies. It was the end of my illusion. At that moment I knew who I was and who they were, and that something separated us. I was very sad. Their world was closed to me. For if among us there was no common present, it was because there was no shared past.

June 5, 1967. My mother's broken voice awakened me from my deep sleep. She stood at the threshold of my bedroom uttering over and over again, *"milchumah, milchumah,"* as if it were a litany. We all expected a war, but when we heard that it began the shock was more devastating than in our wildest imagination. I leaped out of bed, sobbing uncontrollably. I thought for an instant about the morning ritual. It all seemed so silly. What importance could I give to changing into clothes, or washing my face or even eating breakfast? It was meaningless. Everything that day seemed totally meaningless. The reports we heard on the radio as we sat glued to the kitchen table were even more hallucinatory. Could Haifa be burning? Could Netanya be bombed? Then what would happen to Tel Aviv or Jerusalem? We began to imagine the unthinkable.

My mother and I argued, but against whom? We cried to each other — and to God. I could see on my mother's face flashes of the past, a memory of what was, thinking that it could never happen again — or could it? For the first time I saw the nightmare being replayed for my mother and this time I was part of the drama.

The horror began before June 5th. It started in May and lasted throughout the month. The tension was so tight that to relieve it I spent every night at the airport. I heard about the volunteers who left whatever they were doing — work, school, girlfriends, parents — and with a small bag in their hands they took off for Israel. I didn't know of anyone going to Israel, but after I got to the airport there was always a familiar face, somewhere from my past. I was too young to volunteer without permission from my parents. And besides, they would never sign me away to a place where war was imminent.

I remember standing on the observation tower night after night extending my hand outward, groping toward the El Al plane which stood there so alone. At least to touch the Magen David on the tail. Perhaps it would magically transport me to Israel. I watched the volunteers walk toward the plane. Their fearful parents, with eyes swollen with tears, waved goodbye to their messengers. I knew, we all knew, the danger that awaited them. But to me they were luckier, braver. They did something about their fears while I merely lived with mine: each day dreading the next one. How I envied them.

At night it was the airport, by day it was school. I don't know how I lasted through those days in May. At the time there were exams hanging over my head. But they seemed trivial. Logic 101 when sandbags were being filled in Jerusalem? Calculus 5 when shelters were being prepared in the North? Physics 1 when soldiers waved goodbye to their families? Studying didn't make any sense. There we would sit — ten or fifteen of my friends in the lounge, giving each other strength and consolation, while the rest of the students wandered through the campus singing or chatting in the beautiful spring weather.

I had planned my first trip to Israel for the summer of 1967 long before there was talk of war. When the war broke out it seemed like a deliberate punishment for not going sooner. I felt guilty at having those thoughts. Soon guilt turned to grief. If Israel were no longer to exist, I did not want to live either. I would then have to die without ever having seen the land. It would be my punishment for staying here.

Three weeks later I was standing in Lod Airport. My Israeli cousins rushed to greet me, enveloping me with kisses and hugs. I never had seen them before, but they recognized me because I resemble my father and his mother. The next two months were an uninterrupted dream. Israel assaulted my senses. Hot days alternated with cool nights under the canopy of the Jerusalem sky. The sweet scent of green fields filled my nostrils while the touch of sunrise caressed my being.

I returned to Israel the next summer for a year. Then I learned about the texture of the mud and sand, the roughness and softness of the people, the joys and tragedies which bound us all together: the taste of home. I fell deeper in love with the land and its people and realized how I was always there even when I wasn't.

Maybe this was because Israel was never an abstract concept for me. It neither began with theories nor continued with explanations. It was always there, a part of our home, our lives, our souls. Our attachment to Israel was as obvious as our own Jewishness. The plaque of the Old City of Jerusalem which hung above my father's green chair in the living room was as familiar to me as my mother's Sabbath candles. Beneath the plaque was a saying I memorized long before I knew its meaning. "If I forget thee O Jerusalem, let my right hand fail." The warning was serious and stern and I never once took it lightly. Later on when I would think about it, it occurred to me that the punishment for forgetting was the deadening of life. I looked at that hand and imagined it lying there paralyzed because I had forgotten Jerusalem. It was a heavy price to pay for a slip of the memory.

At home there was a large book with a dark blue cover. It commemorated Israel's third birthday. On every shiny page were black and white photographs of Jewish soldiers, modern Jewish cities, Jewish farms. One picture stands out in my mind: the flag of Israel against a clear sky. "That's the Jewish flag," my mother said. I never heard it called Israeli flag, but always the Jewish flag. To me it is still that, a Jewish flag, and always will be that.

We were in constant touch with Israel through letters and holiday greetings. I used to rip off the colorful stamps from the envelopes and place them carefully and neatly in my drawer. The envelopes bore names of people and places I would memorize even before I could differentiate between the people and the places from which they came. They were my parents' relatives and friends who went to Israel after the war. They were all carbon copies of us. And they spoke about Israel with the kind of ease and fervor that was used when speaking about "home." It was never a debate over Zionist ideology — I never knew what Zionism was until I was much older. Rather, it was familiar talk, as if they were living both here and there at the same time.

I conjured up in my mind an image of the place which I was told was my home. It was based on the plaque, the blue book, the stories and the stamps. It was the Garden of Eden — a place I learned in Hebrew school that was full of trees and sunshine and warmth. It never occurred to me as a young child that there was ever a question of loyalty between two places. Those questions came up much later in school among Jews whose parents were American. I knew that Israel was our home, and America was where we lived. As a child I lived with this paradox quite naturally. The contradiction only became apparent when I became much older. Then I had to decide whether my home was what I called home or the place where I spent my days and nights.

As I dreamed of the land I also imagined what a place with all Jews was like. Was it like the summers in the country? Or the Sundays with my parents' friends? Did everybody speak Yiddish? Was it true that I didn't have to sing Christmas songs any longer, nor be called dirty Jew by vengeful Catholic girls? Imagine, I thought, all my friends would be Jewish. It was a simple notion of a Jewish state.

As the years went by, sophistication replaced simplicity. Yet, the attachment grew still stronger. The more Israel entered the depths of my soul the more I understood that my parents were the road over which the journey had occurred. Without their knowing, they had presented me with an inheritance they themselves could not acquire. The war left them tired, beaten. In the German D.P. Camp where I was born there were hundreds of families waiting for a place to go. Years later, I asked my parents why we came to America and why we didn't go to Israel. Even the Zionists were tired, they explained. Idealism was a luxury which was taken from them. They needed a place to begin again, a place where they could bury the wounds and cover the memories. Israel at that time offered them uncertainty, if anything. Had they been single they might have gone to Israel. With a family there were responsibilities. I knew that they really didn't have the choice to go to Israel. It was already made for them. I can only understand. I can't blame them for that.

Today I am at the same age as my parents were when they came to America. And I have chosen to immigrate to Israel, long before I even know how to decide. My father still asks me why I want to go, when things are still so uncertain, so dangerous there. "It's because of you," I answer. My father doesn't understand that I am going for my parents and his parents, and for all the generations of Jews who didn't have the opportunity that I have now.

If I stayed in America, would my children feel the urgency of Jerusalem when they reach my age, as I do now? Would the burden and the duty of the past be as heavy for them as it is for me? Would their lives in America make them forget that which preceded them? And would I be able to teach them what is so very difficult for even me to understand? Would they even want to know?

So, my decision must not only be for me but it must be for my children and their children, and it must be for my parents and their parents. And even when my father argues that it will be difficult, I know that deep down I am doing that which he would have done had the War not stripped him of his choice. He knows it even as he tries to convince me not to go. And I also know that he sees himself in me.

As strong as my desire is to go to Israel, so is the despair I feel at leaving my parents. I will be leaving, and my sister will be leaving for Israel, too. And for the same reasons. I stay up nights imagining the scene at the airport on the day we leave. I ask myself at night when it is quiet and only my heart can speak: is it worth it? Is the land and the idea behind it so important? I will be leaving my parents forever. In place of the intimate joys and problems we have shared, there will only be occasional visits, irregular calls. My children may not even speak the language of my parents. And how will they even know their grandparents? All this I have imposed on a generation not yet born.

Then I recall the legacy of my own generation: what happened thirty years ago imposed a new dimension on the relationship between survivor and child. There is a voice which calls out and tells us that this generation is not like the rest. A voice reminds me of a picture of my mother in the D.P. Camp, pregnant with me, celebrating Israel's birth. It is a voice which tells me of the connection between myself and my parents, between us and Israel, between what happened to them and what I must do for myself. Munich, Lod, Yom Kippur, Maalot, Kiryat Shmonah. These events move closer together. And the further we are from the Holocaust, the more all other tragedies are bound to it.

I realized long ago that I could not share the same stage as others. For me there is always that plaque above my father's chair to remind me of him as well as of Jerusalem. For if I did forget, I now know that more than just my right hand would fail.

"One Generation After," William Aron, Photographer

NOTES ON CONTRIBUTORS

WILLIAM S. ARON has been conducting a two-year in-depth photosociological study of contemporary life in New York's Lower East Side. He is also a staff member of Project Ezra, a local grass roots community organization which serves the Jewish elderly poor.

ENID DAME is a writer living in Brooklyn. "Diaspora 4" originally appeared in the *Jewish Art Quarterly*, which is a student literary magazine at City College, New York.

BETH BRODER EPSTEIN is Adjunct Assistant Professor of English at Rider College, Trenton, where she is faculty co-advisor at Hillel. She is currently preparing an article on anti-Semitism and Chaucer's "The Prioress' Tale," and is researching for a book of children's stories on Jewish themes.

MARCIA FALK teaches Comparative Literature and Hebrew at the State University of New York, Binghamton. Her forthcoming book of poems and translations, *This Year in Jerusalem: 5734*, will be published by Kelsey Street Press in 1976.

MEYER GOLDSTEIN: (See page 33.)

GERSHOM GORENBERG is a Religious Studies major at the University of California, Santa Cruz. He writes poetry and occasional short fiction.

WILLIAM B. HELMREICH teaches sociology and Jewish studies at City College and has written on Black militants, Haiti and the Bowery.

HANS HERDA teaches mathematics at Boston State College. He enjoys pottery, reading and poetry (especially from the T'ang Dynasty). He has recently learned how to weave on a loom.

BARRY IVKER teaches English at Dillard University and is involved in a variety of Jewish adult education programs. His children attend the Hebrew Day School in New Orleans.

ERIC A. KIMMEL is Assistant Professor of Education at Indiana University at South Bend and is the author of novels and stories for children. He has recently completed a novel called *Sabbath Bride* about Shabbetai Tzvi.

YOSSI KLEIN is a columnist for *The Jewish Post and Opinion* and will be making aliya to Israel in 1976. He is a child of Holocaust survivors who grew up in Borough Park, Brooklyn.

LEONARD LEVIN teaches and does free-lance writing on philosophy and Jewish theology. He has just completed a three-year post-doctoral fellowship at the Jewish Theological Seminary of America. He is active in various organs of the Havurah movement.

HANNAH LEVINSKY KOEVARY is a writer and a student in modern Jewish history, whose M.A. thesis is on Franz Kafka and Zionism. She and her husband Tom plan to settle in Israel next year.

LYN LIFSHIN has recently published *the old house, plymouth* (Capra Press, Calif.). Her books *upstate madonna* and the third edition of *black apples* are now available from The Crossing Press, N.Y. Her poems have appeared in numerous anthologies.

TOBY MOSTYSSER teaches college English, studies Hebrew, and is presently working on a book about the impact of the Holocaust on children of survivors.

B. Z. NIDITCH's poetry has recently appeared in the *Revue de Louisione, Wind, Bitterroot, Poems*, and *RESPONSE* magazines. He is working on a selection of poems tentatively called *Joy St. and others*.

ANITA (CHANA) NORICH: (See page 33.)

LILIANE RICHMAN, a native of France, now lectures in French language and literature in Milwaukee. She writes short stories, children's books and poetry.

BOB ROSENBLOOM is presently employed by the U.S. Postal Service. He is trying to break into the field of stand-up comedy and is showcasing around New York City constantly.

DINA ROSENFELD: (see page 33.)

BOB SALZ, a former member of Habonim, is assistant to the editor of the *Jewish Frontier*. He has a master's degree in social studies education from Teachers College, Columbia University.

LUCY Y. STEINITZ: (See page 33.)

DAVID M. SZONYI: (See page 33.)

ERICA WANDERMAN is a doctoral candidate in clinical psychology at New York University, and is the daughter of two Holocaust survivors. Her article is part of a dissertation research project on the effects of concentration camp survival on the second generation.

MICHAEL WATERS has spent this year as Poet-in-Residence for the South Carolina Arts Commission. He is twenty-five. His book *Fish Light* will appear early next year from Ithaca House. "Dachau Moon" was published in the *American Poetry Review*.

ERNA WEILL is a sculptress who works mainly in stone and bronze. Her pieces are exhibited in museums, public institutions and private collections in the United States and abroad. She is a refugee from Nazi Germany.

ROCHELLE SAIDEL WOLK, a field representative for Albany Israel Bond Office, taught art for eight years in New York City and in the Bet Shraga Hebrew Academy, Albany, New York.

MICHAEL WYSCHOGROD is a professor of philosophy at Bernard Baruch College, New York. His fields are contemporary existentialism, philosophy of religion and Jewish thought.

MOSHE YUNGMAN, born in Galicia in 1922, survived the Holocaust and settled in Palestine in 1947. He now lives in Tivon, Israel, where he advises educational programs. He has published five books of poetry in Yiddish, including *Regn-Boign Tzukopns* (*Rainbows at the Head*), from which the two poems here were translated.

DATE DUE

NOV 2 1994	
DEC 05 1994	
DEC 20 1994	
FEB 2 5 1995	
JAN 13 1997	
FEB 13 1997	
FEB 07 2001	
FEB 21 2001	
March 7, 2001	
MAR 19 2001	

GAYLORD   PRINTED IN U.S.A.